ROCK SOLID

12 gospel truths to live by

Edited by Trevor Archer
and Tim Thornborough

D0954596

thegoodbook
COMPANY

Rock Solid: 12 gospel truths to live by
© The Good Book Company 2009
This edition published for Truth for Life, 2013

Edited by Trevor Archer and Tim Thornborough

Published by The Good Book Company
170 W. Main St, Purcellville VA, 20132, USA

Tel: 866 244 2165; International: +1 866 244 2165
Email: sales@thegoodbook.com
www.thegoodbook.com

Websites:
North America: www.thegoodbook.com
UK and Europe: www.thegoodbook.co.uk
Australia: www.thegoodbook.com.au
New Zealand: www.thegoodbook.co.nz

ISBN: 9781906334680

Cover design by Steve Devane

Printed in the USA

CONTENTS

TRUTHFOR**LIFE**®

Truth For Life is the Bible-teaching ministry of Alistair Begg. Our mission is to teach the Bible with clarity and relevance so that unbelievers will be converted, believers will be established, and local churches will be strengthened.

Since 1995, **Truth For Life** has aired a Bible-teaching broadcast on the radio, which is now distributed on 1,628 radio outlets each day, and freely on podcast and on the Truth For Life mobile app. Additionally, a large content archive of full-length Bible-teaching sermons is available for free download at www.truthforlife.org.

Truth For Life also makes full-length Bible-teaching available on CD and DVD. These materials, and also books authored by Alistair Begg, are made available at cost, with no markup, so that price is not a barrier to those seeking a deeper understanding of God's Word.

The ministry connects with listeners at live listener and pastor events and conferences across the U.S. and Canada in cities where the radio program is heard.

Contact Truth For Life

In the U.S.:
PO Box 398000, Cleveland, OH 44139   1.888.588.7884
www.truthforlife.org   letters@truthforlife.org

In Canada:
P.O. Box 19008, Delta, BC V4L 2P8   1.877.518.7884
www.truthforlife.ca   letters@truthforlife.ca

And also at:
www.facebook.com/truthforlife   www.twitter.com/truthforlife

PREFACE

This is the second of a trilogy of books originally published for the London Men's Conventions, aimed at equipping Christian men in the very practical area of applying the gospel to everyday living. Although originally written for men, this particular book has the least in it that is specifically for men, so we hope it will be of help and interest to any group of believers who want to grow in their understanding of the Christian faith.

Rock Solid aims to help us get to grips with twelve great truths that together form the core of what it means to be an evangelical Christian. In order to tell the truth, we must know the truth. This book seeks to help explain and clarify these important and glorious doctrines, or 'themes', of the Bible so that we might be able to teach them to others, and contend for them in the workplace and among our neighbours.

The Introductory Chapter paints the big picture and shows why these foundational truths of the gospel are so important today, and how they are related to each other to provide the 'good deposit' of the Christian faith, as the apostle Paul called it.

There then follow twelve chapters in which the essence of these great Bible themes are explained and applied—with the help of a short Bible study and discussion questions aimed at stimulating our thinking and encouraging our action. Brief contemporary stories of how these particular truths have been used by God, either to bring men to Christ, or to teach them something of His ways in their lives are included in each chapter. We hope that you will find these true stories, together with the cameos of 'famous

Christian men,' who in the history of the church have contended for the particular doctrine, a great encouragement.

This is primarily a book to be worked through. It is written in the hope that it will not simply be read straight through, but, in men's or women's groups, or informal small groups, it will be used as a means of getting a clear hold on the truths that define who we are as followers of Christ.

Tim Thornborough and Trevor Archer

February 2009

INTRODUCTION: WHY IS DOCTRINE SO IMPORTANT?

Richard Coekin

Here are twelve big questions that are the subject of debate in churches and in our culture in general, or which regularly trouble ordinary believers:

★ Will a devout Buddhist be with us in heaven?

★ How can adultery be wrong if it feels so good?

★ Is Jesus' death on the cross an act of 'cosmic child abuse'?

★ Should the Church of England consider joining with the Roman Catholic Church?

★ How can I trust God when my best friend has just died of cancer?

★ How can I tell if my mother is really a Christian?

★ Why shouldn't I watch a little porn?

★ Why does it matter if the Digo tribe in Tanzania have never heard about Jesus?

★ Why are some evangelical Christians so opposed to some church leaders?

★ Should we get rid of sermons in a post-modern culture?

★ Is the little house-church down my street really a church or a dangerous sect?

★ Should practicing homosexuals be allowed to become ministers in the church?

There's a vicious rumour going round that doctrine is boring and irrelevant. Just something for 'theological types' to argue about, and only of passing interest to the man in the pew. If this is what you think, you could not be more wrong.

The answer you might give to each of these twelve current and controversial questions depends on a doctrine. Each one finds an answer in the corresponding chapters of this book; because this book explores twelve of the most relevant and important themes or 'doctrines' of the Bible.

Each one has been treasured and proclaimed down the centuries by Christians known as evangelicals (those concerned to believe and teach the 'evangel' ie: the gospel of the Bible). But each one has also been challenged throughout church history and is still being challenged today.

This book aims to clarify and explain these vital doctrines so that Christian men of our generation will be prepared to stand up and proclaim them: to teach them in our families, our Sunday schools and churches; to contend for them in our church councils, in the office and in the pub; and to ensure they are passed on to the generation after us.

Christian men don't want to be ashamed of the teachings of our Saviour passed on by His prophets and apostles in Scripture, for He said: 'Whoever is ashamed of me and of my words in this sinful and adulterous generation, of him will the Son of Man also be ashamed when he comes in the glory of his Father'(Mark 8 v 38).

We want the whole world to hear and understand the profound truths of the saving gospel announcement that Jesus (the crucified man from Nazareth) is the Christ (the promised Saviour King) and our Lord (the risen divine Ruler and Judge of us all), which are amplified in these twelve 'doctrines'. We need to understand them.

This is vitally important for showing how these themes are not random and isolated ideas, but belong together and sum up the essential teaching of the Bible.

Why are these doctrines important today?

'Doctrines' are principles that summarise the Bible's teaching about particular topical issues. Such principles are enormously helpful in applying the Bible's teaching to the practical issues of real life. I will struggle to find one Bible text to give me a thorough answer to any of the twelve current issues mentioned at the start of this chapter! I need to find some kind of summary of what the Bible as a whole teaches about such questions. These are biblical 'doctrines'.

'Doctrine' is therefore a bit different to the 'exposition' of a Bible text (exploring the meaning of one passage). It is also different to 'Biblical Theology' (exploring how God has developed themes progressively through the different books of the Bible). We do need to use all three approaches in interpreting the Bible. But, if one contrasted these approaches in terms of, say, studying wildlife, 'exposition' is like studying one region of Africa and looking at the variety of animals that happen to be there. 'Biblical theology' is like tracking one animal as it travels across the region. But 'doctrine' is like collecting all the animals of one species together in a game reserve in order to make a comprehensive survey and come to accurate general conclusions about that animal! 'Doctrine' gives us general conclusions about the whole Bible's teaching on particular issues. We all have our own doctrines (ie: our assumptions) about what the whole Bible teaches. The value of a book like this is to try and ensure that our doctrine is accurate and our assumptions are truly biblical.

Now, bad doctrine is crushingly dull. Sometimes it becomes so over-systematised that it seems to be more human construction than biblical summary—so it is important to keep involving what the Bible actually says in how we articulate our doctrines.

Sometimes doctrine becomes so swamped in historical debates that it seems more like church history than what the Bible teaches (so we must keep returning to what the Bible teaches, rather than what church leaders have said). Sometimes doctrine is employed so much in criticising others that it seems more about dividing up the 'tribes' of Christianity than about understanding God's uniting word (so it's vital to be humble about our doctrinal conclusions, gentle in how we express them and joyful in recognising Christians from other backgrounds who are united with us in these truths).

Good doctrine is, however, invaluable. It is helpful in providing a sense of proportion and perspective to our understanding of Scripture, especially for inexperienced Christians. This prevents us overemphasising minor themes and underemphasising major principles. It is helpful in providing the background or context for interpreting any part of the Bible. This is especially helpful in understanding the more difficult texts. It is also enormously helpful for giving us general principles for making the countless moral decisions we have to make each day. And doctrine is vital for finding ways to express the faith of the Bible in language that ordinary people can understand! Good doctrine is truly invaluable.

How do these doctrines help describe evangelical faith?

Some people object to defining 'evangelical' doctrines at all. They plead that we just describe ourselves as 'Christian' and leave labels to others. We can all sympathise with this desire. It's ugly to use terminology for making assumptions about people or chucking slogans at them in criticism. However, we still need labels and to learn how to use them lovingly.

The term 'evangelical' is a helpful name for a generally recognised set of doctrines. If we can't use any labels, we end up having to list what we believe in great detail every time we want to join with other Christians in initiatives. Or else we become needlessly suspicious that everyone else believes different things. Young children don't like big words, but as we grow up we learn to use terminology and labels in every area of thinking and communication. Christianity is no different. As we grow in our responsibility for others and our desire to help others, we have to find terminology and labels for different beliefs.

Some say that the name 'evangelical' is no longer useful! Certainly, some people are describing themselves as Evangelical who wouldn't agree with many of the principles explained in this book! But most Christians still use this label and, until a better one becomes widely used, this book will hopefully contribute some clarity to what the label has generally been understood to include over centuries.

It's worth recording that all the contributors to this book are passionate believers in, and open teachers of, all the doctrines considered in this book. While we would all debate the finer points and the precise ways of explaining these doctrines, we are united in these truths! The truth does distinguish error, but it is also the focus for our unity!

The doctrines explored in this book are, however, not a complete summary of evangelical faith e.g. there's nothing here specifically about Creation or the Trinity, which evangelicals certainly believe!

These twelve doctrines have been chosen because they are important truths which have all been challenged at various times by different groups and are strongly contested today. Indeed, one recent survey of British Anglican clergy reports that roughly a quarter do not believe that Christ died on the cross for our sins, a third do not believe that Jesus rose bodily from His grave, and nearly half do not believe that Jesus is the only way of salvation! These are twelve doctrines that in successive generations have been defended and clarified as vital biblical truths that must not be surrendered.

The depravity of sin

Justification of believers by grace alone

The unique supremacy of Christ

The penal substitution of Christ

The necessity of holiness

The sovereignty of God the Father

EVANGELICAL FAITH

The regeneration of God the Holy Spirit

The importance of the local church

The priority of evangelism

The centrality of Bible teaching

The reality of judgment

The authority of Scripture

They are therefore like some sections of the castle ramparts of biblical faith which are under constant attack from the enemies of the gospel—other sections will no doubt have to be defended in future generations. These doctrines help clarify what genuine evangelicals believe. Other Christians would believe some of them, but only evangelical Christians believe all these doctrines consistently. But these are not a complete statement of all that we believe. Evangelicals also believe all that the Bible teaches because this is well summarised in the historic creeds such as the Nicene and Apostles' creeds, which are recited in many churches each Sunday. But the doctrines in this book are biblical truths which evangelicals have always believed, and which others have repeatedly disputed and still dispute today.

It has been rightly said that evangelical faith is trying to be no more and no less than the faith expressed in the Bible. Our church traditions (what others have previously worked out in church history), our rational thinking (what we think the Bible means), and our reflection upon our experiences (trying to work out what is happening to us according to the Bible) help us to understand the text of the Bible. This means we only believe what the Bible says about God.

An evangelical will not accept ideas about God that contradict or go beyond the plain teachings of Scripture. Evangelicals will humbly try to adapt our traditions, rational thinking and experiences to what the Bible plainly says. Someone who accepts the traditions of the Church and its councils beyond the Bible, or even revises the faith of the Bible, could be described as 'traditionalist' (such as Roman Catholics). Someone who allows modern rational thought about God to go beyond the Bible, or even to revise the Bible's teaching, could be described as 'rationalist' (such as liberals). Someone who allows reflection upon our experiences to go beyond what the Bible says, or even revises what the Bible says, could be described as 'subjectivist' (such as some charismatics). Such people will, of course, still be real Christians if they are trusting the central gospel message of Scripture that Jesus Christ is Lord, as evident in His incarnation, death for our sins, resurrection to rule and return to judge. For more on this see Men of God, available from The Good Book Company.

But if teaching about God goes beyond or even revises what God has revealed in Jesus as He is revealed in Scripture, then this is not true teaching. For instance, those who assume that there are many religious ways to God are allowing their rational ideas to go beyond the Bible, where Jesus said, 'No-one comes to the Father except by me!' (John 14 v 6) This is rationalism.

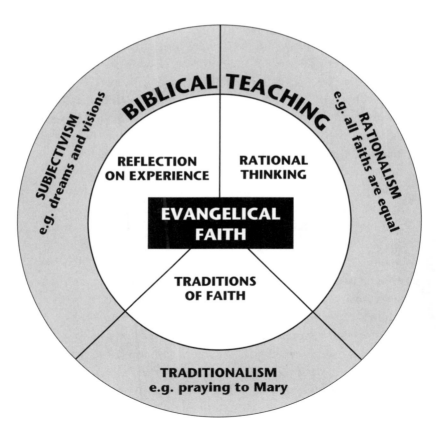

Those who assume from traditions established by church councils in the past, that we can pray to Mary or to the saints to mediate for us go beyond the Bible which says: 'There is one mediator between God and man, the Jesus Christ'. (1 Timothy 2 v 5) This is traditionalism.

Those who assume that dreams and visions contain messages from God are going beyond the Bible, which says: 'Long ago, at many times and in many ways, God spoke to our fathers by the prophets, but in these last days he has spoken to us by his Son.' (Hebrews 1 v 1). The Bible is the 'lamp shining in a dark place' (2 Peter 1 v 19), which is God's lamp to our feet to guide us. To go beyond this is really 'subjectivism' even though many lovely Christians seem to be in the habit of doing this.

It is vital to remember, however, that none of us understands perfectly or holds purely to the doctrines of Scripture. Each of us is a mix of beliefs, some from the Bible, some from wrong traditions, ideas and reflections upon experience, and some from frankly worldly, sinful thinking. Those of us who claim to be evangelical may well be less obedient and pleasing to Jesus, despite all our good doctrine, than others who are less informed but more obedient to what they know!

Even where we are willing to be taught by the Scriptures, we will always be 'work in progress'; and we will sometimes describe ourselves inaccurately. We need to be careful about the labels we use of ourselves and others. We need to remember that, even if someone has some strange beliefs, if they believe the gospel, they are still our Christian brothers and sisters and we must love them generously.

The twelve doctrines considered in this book are arranged historically (ie: roughly in the order in which they were either mostly seriously challenged or most clearly explained in church history), so as to give a sense of the story of our evangelical heritage. This reminds us that these are not strange or novel ideas. They are orthodox truths that evangelicals have believed since the coming of Christ. But the order is a little artificial in that each generation has believed all of these doctrines (because they are biblical) but with varying emphases (because each generation has different challenges and different weaknesses).

We have also selected, for each period, a champion defender of the doctrine. This adds some personal colour to the debates but should also alert us to the wonderful writings of different generations, which are often so helpful in correcting blind spots of our own. This will help us recognise, with humility, the debts we owe to those who wrestled and often suffered for the acceptance of doctrines which are widely recognised as biblical today. However, we should remember that these were not the only men who taught these doctrines. Some, such as Calvin and Owen, taught most of them very clearly and others were seriously flawed in other areas of their teaching. But we all have much to learn from these great ones (and hopefully we'll be inspired to read some good biographies on holiday).

How do these doctrines relate to each other: an 'Executive Summary'

We should briefly consider each of the doctrines explained in this book to see how they fit together. They are consistent with each other and interdependent—that is to say, if we abandon one of them, then we will soon begin to lose the others, rather as unpicking one thread can gradually unravel a whole sweater.

For example, if we abandon belief in God's punishment of sin, then there is no need to think of Jesus suffering our punishment in His death. If Jesus didn't suffer the punishment for our sins, then Jesus would not be the only way of salvation and clearly sin is not as serious as we thought, and holiness could hardly be necessary. If holiness is not necessary, then why would regeneration by the Holy Spirit of God really be required? These doctrines fit together and depend on each other, and therefore we cannot surrender any of them lightly.

Reference is also made here to the important issues mentioned at the beginning of this chapter, to remind us of how relevant today these doctrines are:

1. The unique supremacy of Christ

This is a distinctive view of Jesus. The Bible teaches that Jesus did not merely claim to be a prophet or super-human. He is not merely the best of many ways to God. He is uniquely and eternally God the Son, now fully human as well. He is the complete and unique self-revelation of God. He is the complete and uniquely true and living way to be saved by God. He is now risen and enthroned at the right hand of the Father as supreme Lord to rule and judge us all.

This doctrine is vital in an increasingly pluralistic culture, that believes that many religions lead to God. This means that devout Buddhists will not be in heaven unless they turn to Christ in repentance and faith.

The reason that we needed this uniquely supreme Saviour is because of:

2. The seriousness of sin

This is a distinctive view of humanity. The Bible teaches that we share the guilt of the original rebellion of our representative ancestor, Adam. We are also guilty of enjoying our slavery to the world's hostile rebellion against God, to Satan's influence to distrust God's word, and to our nature's proud and selfish desires. We are not only corrupted in our physical desires but also in our perception and wills.

We all, therefore, naturally suppress our awareness of God from creation and conscience. We prefer instead the idolatrous versions of Him found in the spiritual ideologies of man (which we call religious!). We are all naturally dead to God and deserving of His eternal condemnation and just punishment in hell.

This doctrine is vital in a culture that imagines that we are beautiful in every single way and acceptable just the way we are. This also explains why adultery can seem good to us and yet is really utterly wicked according to God.

To rescue us from this deserved wrath of God we therefore need:

3. The penal substitution of Christ's death

This is a distinctive view of the death of Christ. The Bible teaches that, just as a football substitute takes the place of a player on the pitch, so Jesus took our place on the cross in 'substitution' for us. It was 'penal' in that He suffered there the penalty, or punishment, for our sin. God did this to satisfy His own personal justice.

This means that Christ's death not only conquered Satan and his power of death... not only set us an example of sacrificial love to follow... but, supremely, satisfied God for our sins. His death was the pleasing sacrifice for our cleansing from corruption (as modelled in the temple system). His death was the price for our ransom from slavery (as modelled in the redemption of Israel from Egypt). His obedience unto death was the righteousness to secure our acceptance or justification (as modelled in the legal system).

This doctrine is vital in a culture where we fondly imagine that God could just overlook our faults and not bother about our sin. It also means that the view that the cross is an example of 'cosmic child abuse' is simply wrong, because the Bible teaches that 'he was wounded for our transgressions.'

Only on the basis of such a death could God justly provide:

4. The justification of believers by grace alone

This is a distinctive view of our salvation. The Bible teaches that we are acceptable to God, and reckoned righteous or 'justified' in His judgment, only by the righteousness of Christ's perfect obedience counted as ours. This is not because of anything good in us ie: it is by the generosity of His 'grace' alone.

Christ 'swapped' places with us: God the Father treated Jesus just-as-if-He-was-me (and punished Him) so that He can treat me 'just-as-if-I'd' been Jesus (and can accept or 'justify' me). By faith in Jesus, we have already received God's judgement declaration that we are acceptable to Him, not because of God's work in us by His Spirit or through the sacraments or by our service, but solely because of His work in Christ as a loving gift to us. Jesus lived the Christian life I cannot live. His resurrection demonstrated that His life was acceptable for our justification for every day of our lives. This sets us free to serve God not in order to be saved but because we have already been saved in Christ.

This doctrine is vital in a culture where religion is imagined to be the burden of being good in order to get saved. It also means that the protestant churches could never unite with the Roman Catholic church because they can never agree in this doctrine.

Such a salvation by God's gracious initiative is only possible because of:

5. The sovereignty of God the Father

This is a distinctive view of history. The Bible teaches that God created the world and governs every detail of history, including the salvation of the sinners that He has elected to save for eternity. The future is not uncertain or at risk to God, as some suggest!

We can only know the part of His plans that He has published in the Scriptures. But all who have been called by God through the gospel are assured that God is at work in all things, however painful and confusing some will be, toward His good purpose of our becoming like Christ. He will keep us persevering to the end, for He chose and predestined us from before the creation of the world to share His glory. Indeed, none of us would have any chance of being saved had He not done so. These are truths to reassure worried Christians, and not for speculating about who may or may not have been chosen. Knowing that God has chosen to save many, we preach the gospel to everyone that will listen.

This doctrine is vital in a culture that believes we are at the mercy of fate, that God can't direct history, or that we are the controllers of our own destinies. It also means that I can still trust God to be working His purposes out even when my best friend has just died of cancer.

This salvation in Christ is applied personally to us through:

6. The regeneration of God the Holy Spirit

This is a distinctive view of Christian experience. The Bible teaches that God creates new life in us, not through baptism but through His gospel. Through God's word, God's Spirit creates the faith to believe His word and to repent or turn from sin. He indwells every Christian, bringing new life and a love for keeping the law of Christ. He helps us to know Christ, to speak of Christ, to serve one another like Christ, to bear the fruit of Christlikeness and to pray to our Father as Christ did.

The supreme blessing of life under the 'new covenant' (promise or arrangement) of the gospel is to enjoy the presence of the Spirit of God Himself within us, transforming us gradually through His word to become fitting residences for the living God and uniting us by faith into Jesus Himself.

This doctrine, that we must be 'born again' by the Holy Spirit, is vital in a culture that thinks Christianity is a superficial lifestyle choice we make for ourselves. It also means that I can tell if my mother is really a Christian by her devotion to Christ.

The urgent necessity of this priceless salvation by God derives from:

7. The reality of God's coming judgment

This is a distinctive view of the future. The Bible teaches that Christ will return to raise all humanity to face His judgment. He will welcome all who have trusted the gospel about Him into the eternal paradise-kingdom of the new creation. All who don't know God, or have failed to believe His gospel, will forever be excluded from His presence in the ruinous destruction of eternally just and conscious punishment. There will be no 'purgatory' or further chances for repentance. Those who have never heard of Christ will not be condemned for rejecting Christ (for they have never heard of Him), but for rejecting their Creator, of whom they were aware from creation and conscience, but preferred religious alternatives to Him.

We can only consider such sombre truths with tears and heavy hearts but we are not at liberty to change the teachings of Scripture—even if they are politically incorrect.

This doctrine is vital in a culture that doesn't believe in resurrection or our accountability to God. It also means that I mustn't watch even a little porn, because the gospel insists that Christ will one day judge the secrets of our hearts and Christians will receive rewards for our service of Him.

It is this reality that has for generations driven evangelicals to the conviction of:

8. The priority of evangelism

This is a distinctive view of the world we live in. The Bible teaches that as Christ turned from concentrating on healing to focus upon preaching the gospel, and as His apostles delegated their famine relief so as not to be distracted from their ministries of prayer and the word, so we must recognise that the kindest and most loving thing that we can do for a poor and needy world is to proclaim the gospel.

Of course, evangelicals have always also served the social needs of their societies. We aren't able to preach all the time. It is our love that so often opens people's ears to our message, and it is inherently good to serve people and to contribute to the government of God's creation in accordance with His word. But our highest priority is spreading the news about Jesus. Even more terrible than the awful tragedy of AIDS and the injustice of famine is the wrath to come and the starving spiritual needs for the bread of life evident everywhere in our world.

When there is competition for our time, money and energy we sometimes have to make painful choices. Evangelicals have recognised that we are here to maximise what we can do, as the people we are, with the gifts and opportunities that God has entrusted to us, to advance the work of teaching the gospel of Christ far and wide. The world won't understand or praise our commitment to missionary priorities, but they are the priorities of Jesus.

This is a vital doctrine in a culture that thinks the world's greatest needs are for health and happiness now. It also means that the greatest kindness we can do for the Digo people of Tanzania is give them the gospel in their own language, and if necessary to take it there ourselves.

The authority by which we address the nations with this gospel comes from:

9. The authority of Scripture

This is a distinctive view of how we know God. The Bible teaches that as Christ regarded every word of the Old Testament as the voice of God 'today', reliable and authoritative in every detail, so Christians should listen to the voice of God today, addressing us in the sentences of the Scriptures (the Old Testament fulfilled with the New Testament writings of Christ's authorised, apostolic eye-witnesses). Interpreted in accordance with its various kinds of literature (including literary conventions such as approximation, poetic devices and the personal emphases of different authors) the Bible is without error in all it affirms.

Moreover, since the Bible is God's complete summary of the person and work of Christ, it contains everything we could possibly need to know from God for salvation and righteousness. The Spirit of God guides us through the word of God which is the light to our paths, so that we may be thoroughly equipped for every good work.

The Bible carries authority over our own ideas, experiences and traditions including the leaders and councils of churches. None of us interprets the Bible perfectly. But God created us to understand His language, gives us His own Spirit to help us understand Him, and revealed Himself in Christ in the Scriptures perfectly to enable us to grow in our personal relationship with Him.

This doctrine is vital in a culture that believes it is impossible to know God certainly or personally. It also means that church leaders who believes Scripture is merely the unreliable reflections of the disciples are bound to be challenged by evangelicals.

This understanding of the Bible results in practice in:

10. The centrality of Bible-teaching

This is a distinctive view of Christian ministry. The preaching and teaching of God's word is not simply the preferred option of certain kinds of intellectual churches. The Bible is how the Spirit of God grows and directs His churches and His people.

As the Scriptures are taught in Sunday School, youth events, congregational meetings, outreach and missionary initiatives, the Spirit of God is calling the people of God to faith and repentance. He is giving new life, judging sin and approving righteousness, making holy and strengthening His people so that they can go out to live lives of sacrificial worship. The exposition of Bible passages in the light of the biblical theological themes progressing through Scripture and the summary doctrines of the Bible is the engine of life in evangelical churches. It is not our informality or our management or our personalities that grows genuine churches in size and maturity. It is the faithful and passionate preaching of God's word that everyone should submit to.

This doctrine is vital in a culture that prefers us to provide unchallenging entertainment to constantly applaud ourselves. It also means that, far from abandoning our sermons, we want to encourage our ministers to work harder than ever to make them faithful, clear and well-applied. And we will all listen humbly, intelligently, and with a desire to repent and believe.

The power of Bible-teaching explains:

11. The importance of the local church

This is a distinctive view of church. The voice of God in the Scriptures gathers the people of God around the word of God into the church of God. All God's people are in Christ and therefore gathered in the heavenly church around the throne of God. This gathering is reflected on earth in the congregations of God's people gathering to hear God's word.

Denominations and other federations can be helpful but are not strictly churches, and their officers are not strictly the bishops or elders of the local church (even though they may be worthy of great respect for their biblical faithfulness, godliness and wisdom). It is the local church that, by its mutual love and unity in the truth of the gospel, displays the power of God in drawing people together under the rule of Christ and which has responsibility for upholding the truth in this godless generation. It is the distinctive community lives of Christ's churches that will attract unbelievers to consider the gospel.

This doctrine is vital in a culture that assumes that Christianity is like other religions and looks for mysterious ceremony, impressive buildings, and celebrity leaders to find our God, when in fact His power is evident in the ordinary life of our churches. It also means that the smallest house-church that opens the Bible and teaches the gospel is more the house of God than the grandest cathedral.

The witness of the churches to the holy character of God helps explain:

12. The necessity of holiness

This is a distinctive view of the worship that pleases God. Christ died to purify for Himself a people that are His very own, eager to do good. We are warned not to be deceived by those who turn the grace of God into a licence for immorality. We must be clear that those who continue without repentance in wicked lifestyles such as greed, slandering others, or sexual immorality such as homosexual practice are not being saved. Our reasonable worship in response to the gospel is to offer our bodies as living sacrifices, holy and pleasing to God. We all fail and struggle.

We must strive to be holy not in order to be saved, but because we have been saved; and while we are saved not by works but by faith in His works, nevertheless, real faith will always be evident in the growing holiness of God's children, that reflects the holiness of our heavenly Father. This is particularly important to understand and fight for in the present permissive climate of our culture that is compromising so many church leaders across our nation and the western world.

This doctrine is vital in a pleasure-obsessed culture that resents any moral restriction of sexual behaviour. It also means that a man who does not repent of having practised homosexuality, but teaches it as acceptable to God, should never be appointed to any office in a Christian church or denomination.

This last doctrine brings us right up to date with the current debates about Christian lifestyle. It is self-evident that these themes fit with each other, follow from each other and depend on each other. Evangelical faith is not an arbitrary collection of random beliefs but part of the one truth from God Himself.

Conclusion

These are glorious truths to be trusted, proclaimed and celebrated; it would be appropriate to turn aside in prayer to thank God for each of them in turn.

★ These doctrines as they are explained in the ensuing chapters would make useful study subjects for a series of twelve men's meetings or the programme for weekends away.

★ These doctrines are also worth fighting for and indeed, as some have had to do in the past, even dying for! As Luther, the champion of justification by grace alone once wrote:

'If I profess with the loudest voice and clearest exposition every portion of the truth of God except precisely that little point that the world and the devil are at that moment attacking, I am not confessing Christ, however boldly I may be professing Christ. Where the battle rages fiercely is where the loyalty of the soldier is proved, and to be steady on all the battlefield besides is merely flight and disgrace if he flinches at that point.'

May we not flinch but encourage each other to stand up and lovingly proclaim these glorious doctrines. To God alone be all the glory.

1 IS JESUS 'THE ONE AND ONLY'?

The unique supremacy of Christ

Trevor Archer

I s Christianity just one of many alternatives on offer in our world of lifestyle choices? No, says this first doctrine, because Jesus Christ is Lord of all...

Being unique doesn't make you supreme. Every human being is unique but the longer we live the more we appreciate how very vulnerable and weak we are.

Being supreme doesn't make you unique. Great men have their day but ultimately, on the vast scale of time, it is only a 'day'; then along comes another 'great one' to take the crown.

But in Jesus Christ, the supreme Lord of all and unique Son of God, the two come together. Hence the phrase 'the unique supremacy of Christ'.

He is truly Unique: there has never been another human being like Jesus, nor will there ever be. He is truly Supreme, for He is the one who has 'all authority and power' over creation, over history, over life and over the future. That's the astonishing teaching of the Bible and the outrageous claim of Jesus Himself, that separates Christianity from every other world religion—and ultimately and invariably, brings it to loggerheads with every other life-view or belief system.

Consider the extraordinary position claimed for Christ in these five stages of the Bible's storyline:

1. The Creator

The human race did not bring itself into being; we are the creation of God, or to be precise, of Christ the Son. 'Through Him all things were made; without Him nothing was made that has been made' (John 1 v 3)—a pretty comprehensive statement that led one Jehovah's Witness I know to Christ when he grasped its implications—that nobody made Jesus—He is God the Creator.

In Colossians 1 v 15 Christ is described as 'the firstborn of all creation'. Just as in the biblical world the firstborn had certain privileges and rights, so too does Jesus when it comes to the created world—He has first claim, He is pre-eminent, sovereign. Not only is He the origin of all things—'by him all things were created' (Colossians 1 v 16)—He is the one who keeps the whole cosmos ticking over—'in him all things hold together' (Colossians 1 v 17). The fact that the world keeps turning and we keep living is ultimately down to Jesus! Some claim!

And when Christ stepped into His world, He displayed all the power and authority you would expect of the Creator if He came to earth. He demonstrated effortless control over all creation—over nature, over disease, over men, even over death! As the disciples put it: 'Who is this? Even the wind and the waves obey him!' (Mark 4 v 41)

2. The Revealer of God

Left to himself, man cannot answer the big questions about God: Is there a God? What is He like? Can I know Him? If God is invisible, how can we get in contact with Him? That's why there are so many religions in the world, all seeking to make sense of life and provide answers to the big questions of our existence. But, in essence, all religions are about man trying to claw his way up to God, reaching out into the unknown, fumbling about in the dark, inventing gods and deities in a futile attempt to make sense of life. What is needed is not religion, but revelation!

Christ is just that. 'He is 'the image of the invisible God' (Colossians 1 v 15). If you want to know who God is and what He is about, the answer is—look at Jesus! He has come to make God known to all mankind. He is the Word (John 1). Just as our words reveal who we are and explain what is on our hearts, so Christ speaks and reveals the very heart and mind of God (John 14 v 10).

The fact is, God is not hiding from mankind: 'Whoever has seen me has seen the Father' (John 14 v 9). He has not left mankind in the dark. In Christ, He has opened up the conversation, He has come seeking mankind. By His words and deeds, His perfect character and sublime life, Christ shows us exactly who God is and what He is like. 'God was pleased to have all his fullness dwell in Christ' (Colossians 1 v 19). Christianity is a revelation, not a religion—and Christ is THE Revealer of the true God, God's final and complete Word on the matter.

3. The Saviour of Men

However, Jesus didn't come simply to reveal the way to God but to rescue us for God. Our problem is much more serious than simply being lost—we are hopelessly unfit to meet God. Our sin, our pride, our wilful rebellion and shameful actions mean that, even if we could find our way to God (which we can't!), we would be horrified to discover His burning anger against our sin and the utter perfection of His character.

Spiritually, it's not a matter of a mere common cold that's not too serious—we have a cancer of the soul that's deadly. Left to ourselves, there is no way we can cure the problem. But none of the religions on offer in the global hypermarket of today's pluralism take seriously the awful condition of the human heart. They teach that man is essentially OK and by a variety of ritual or rules, sacrifices or self denial, good works or going on pilgrimages, can get right with God. They are all DIY solutions—very appealing but very appalling!

The Bible is far more realistic. It says that spiritually we are blind (2 Corinthians 4 v 4), and rebellious God haters (Romans 5 v 10) who loathe the thought of God's light shining into our lives (John 3 v 20), that our hearts are rotten at the core (Matthew 15 v 19) and, to cap it all, we are spiritually dead! (Ephesians 2 v 1). Left to ourselves we are in a desperate, hopeless condition, 'having no hope and without God in the world' (Ephesians 2 v 12). A Rescuer is our only hope, a Saviour is our desperate need—which is exactly why Christ came into the world (Luke 19 v 10).

Jesus is not one way back to God, he is the only way (John 14 v 6). He is not one saviour among many. He is the only Saviour. 'Salvation is found in no one else, for there is no other name under heaven given among men by which we must be saved' (Acts 4 v 12). His cross closes the door on any other route, any other Saviour.

4. The risen Lord

Not surprisingly, no religious leader in the history of the world has ever sought to prove his claims to be from God on the basis that if you kill him he will return from the grave—none except Jesus that is! It's a pretty decisive method!

Jesus said: 'Destroy this temple, and in three days I will raise it up' (John 2 v 19). As one of 500 eye-witnesses to the resurrection of Jesus, the apostle Peter laid his own life on the line in proclaiming to those who had crucified Christ: 'You put him to death by nailing him to the cross, but God raised him from the dead' (Acts 2 v 23-24).

The evidence for the resurrection of Christ is overwhelming. The New Testament takes that evidence to show the implications of this great fact of history, namely, that by the resurrection Christ is declared Lord (Romans 1 v 4), the guarantee of all of God's promises (Hebrews 7 v 22), the new Adam, the first of God's new humanity (1 Corinthians 15 v 22, 45), that all authority in heaven and earth has been given to Him (Matthew 28 v 18) so that right now He rules over all (Revelation 1 v 5) as the rightful heir of all things (Hebrews 1 v 2-4).

5. Judge of all mankind

Parents, employers, politicians, generals—all know the importance of the issue: 'Who has the last word?' However the biggest issue is: 'Who has the last word on the history of the world, the destiny of mankind?' In the end the one who has the last word is the only one who matters, who is truly the Boss!

The resurrection is God's great marker in history that declares that Jesus will have the last word (Acts 17 v 31). He has entrusted the judgement of the world to His Son. He alone will determine men's eternal destinies. 'Heaven and earth will pass away but my word will never pass away' (Luke 21 v 33). So we find that the one who has the first word on the world as its Creator will also have the last word as its Judge.

The challenges before us

The Bible presents us with a breathtaking view of the supremacy of Christ and of His unique place at the centre of the universe. But to hold to and declare the Bible's view of who Jesus is will always be tough going. Opposition will come both from a world that is opposed to Him (John 15 v 18-20) and a false church that is ashamed by the exclusiveness of His claims (Mark 8 v 38). So don't be surprised; it's only what He said would happen!

Opposition from 'outside': In these days of religious pluralism it is considered arrogant, narrow-minded and bigoted for Christians to contend that the only path to God is through Jesus. It flies in the face of the dogma of 'tolerance' and appears to be a verbal slap in the face of other belief systems. But the issue remains: 'Is Jesus who He said He is?' (John 14 v 6). Christianity stands and falls on the person and claims of Christ. To paraphrase

C.S.Lewis: 'You must choose: he is an impostor, a madman or the Son of God!'

Mankind will never be comfortable with the Jesus of the Bible simply because His gospel humbles man and His cross declares very simply: nobody is good enough for God, and nobody can earn their salvation. That message is deeply offensive to the pride of man and the political correctness of our day. No wonder it provokes such antagonism and opposition. It's what the Bible calls 'the offence of cross' (Galatians 5 v 11).

Opposition from 'inside': As Christians, we expect to be at war with the world, but when the opposition comes from within the church, from those who profess to be Christ's followers, that is somehow harder to take. It undermines the cause of Christ and brings confusion and derision upon the gospel. But we ought not be surprised. It's not new. Read the New Testament; remember Jesus and the apostles warned about false prophets and false shepherds. Review the stories in this book of great men in history who often had to contend for the apostolic 'faith once delivered' against false teachers; draw heart from their stand, learn from their lives and writings.

Finally, two responses every Christian can make:

1. Commit to Christ as the only Lord
The Christian life flows out of the character of God revealed in Jesus. First and foremost, we are called into relationship with Him to serve Him as our King.

Every day the culture we 'breathe in' will be pressing other claims on our lives. The idols of career, sex, success, materialism and so on will be ever before us, claiming our allegiance and demanding our worship. Daily we need to bring our minds, hearts and wills under His supremacy and that of His word. As the old saying goes, when it comes to our own relationship with Jesus 'either He is Lord of all or not at all'.

Seeing who He is and what He has done for us, how can we do other than give Him lordship over every area our life?

2. Contend for Christ as the only Saviour

Whether it's the false idols of the atheists or the fake gods of the religious, we will find ourselves having to contend for Christ daily in all sorts of situations. The more we know of Christ, the more we will want to speak of Him. Graciously and patiently but firmly and boldly, in the awareness that without Christ people are lost— forever. If all that the Bible teaches about this unique Christ is true, what does it matter what others think of me? One thing's for

BIBLE STUDY

Read Colossians 1 v 15-23

In verses 15-17 Christ is seen to be head over the whole of creation, the visible and the invisible.

Q1. What does the visible and invisible include here?

Q2. What comfort is this meant to be for the Christian (see also v 21-23)?

In verse 18 Christ is supreme over the church, which is God's new creation.

Q3. Why do you think the imagery of 'the body' is used in this instance to describe the church?
What are the implications?

In verses 19-20 Christ is supreme in his saving work for the Christian.

Q4. What should our response be to Jesus Christ, and how are we to show it (v 21-23)?

ATHANASIUS
296-373

The deity of Christ

Three hundred years after Jesus, the church suddenly split down the middle. At issue was the question whether Jesus was really divine. In the great city of Alexandria (Egypt), a new teaching held that Jesus was not eternally one with God but instead a created being. 'There was a time when he was not,' claimed its leader, Arius. Only the Father was truly God.

Arianism quickly won a big following. It seemed to defend the uniqueness and transcendence of God. And it made sense to people who thought God was by definition incapable of sharing His nature. Jehovah's Witnesses take a similar line today.

It fell to another Alexandrian, Athanasius, to spend his life fighting this dangerous error. When he was a young minister, he saw the Council of Nicaea (325 AD) refute Arius. Nicaea insisted that Jesus Christ was 'begotten, not made'; that He was 'true God from true God'; and, crucially, that He was 'of one substance with the Father', sharing the very nature of God.

Far from settling the matter, Nicaea divided the church for half a century. Athanasius grasped how much was at stake, and resisted attempts to rehabilitate the Arians. And unlike his opponents, it was the Bible, not philosophical ideas about God, which shaped his convictions.

Salvation was lost, Athanasius pointed out, if Christ was less than fully God. According to the Bible, Jesus was not a created be-ing—he had been the Father's Son eternally, sharing His nature fully. Since only God can save, this was indispensable as well as true. Because death is the penalty for sin, salvation has to come through the conquest of death by a man. Hence the need for God Himself to become man:

'No one else but the Saviour Himself, who at the beginning made everything Himself out of nothing, could bring the corrupted to incorruption, for no one else but the image of the Father could recreate men in God's image; no one else could make the mortal immortal... Two miracles happened at once: the death of all men was accomplished in the Lord's body, and death and corruption were destroyed because of the Word who was united with it.'

Athanasius suffered for his beliefs, spending seventeen years in exile. At times he felt he stood alone against the world. But his stand saved biblical Christianity, and ensured the church contin-ued to worship and serve Jesus Christ as its Lord and God.

Peter Ackroyd

real lives

'NOT JUST A PROPHET'

Sakhr Namarai ('Zak') was born in Jerusalem and brought up as a Muslim. However it was only when he arrived at university in Edinburgh that he really started thinking about life's big questions and he resolved to look into Islam properly.

He spent the next three and a half years reading the Koran daily, memorising scripture, chatting to Muslim friends, attending the mosque and fasting regularly. But the more he looked into Islam, the more distressed he became.

'The Koran says that your good deeds are weighed against your bad deeds, but the more I tried to make myself acceptable to God, the more I realised I was failing and that I would never get into heaven. The assurance I was searching for just put me under more and more pressure.'

Zak became deeply depressed and when a friend of his suggested he read the Bible—something he would never have considered before—he said yes, almost despite himself.

'We read Psalm 23 first and then John 3 v 16 and I was just totally amazed. This was exactly what I'd been searching for over the past years. I couldn't put the Bible down and, as I read through the Gospels, I started to grasp that Jesus wasn't just a prophet as I had been taught, but that He was unique—in His claims, His prophecies, His teaching, the miracles He performed, everything.

One verse in particular stuck in my mind: 'I am the way, the truth and the life. No one comes to the Father except by me.' At that point I realised that I had to make a choice. Islam and Christianity can't co-exist. Islam disagrees fundamentally that Christ could be a sacrifice for sin, yet the whole message of the Bible seems to rest on that claim. In the end it was the Koran versus the Bible and for me, the evidence of the Bible was so clear, so compelling, so obviously the word of God, that it went straight to my heart.' Zak committed his life to Christ two weeks later.

Since becoming a Christian Zak has had to face the disappointment and opposition of his friends and family, but has stood firm in his faith. 'The hardest thing was admitting that my family is wrong and that I had been wrong for all those years. The Koran is full of wise writing, but ultimately it doesn't deal with our sin, and I have learnt from bitter experience that if I try to earn my way into heaven I will fail.

'Now that my faith is in Christ and in what he has already done on the cross I finally have the assurance I sought for all those years.'

DISCUSS

Q1. What has struck you about the supremacy of Christ that you had not realised before?

Q2. What particular areas of your life do you struggle with in giving over to the lordship of Jesus?

Q3. What kind of people and situations do you find hardest in seeking to share the uniqueness of Jesus and the gospel?

Q4. How can you help yourself and another Christian to be ready and prepared to speak clearly about Christ to someone of another 'faith'?

2 "I'M NOT SUCH A BAD BLOKE DEEP DOWN"

The depravity of sin

Mike Ovey

F rank Sinatra. Wonderful singer, but no great shakes at grasping human nature. One of his theme songs was My Way, a number that celebrates human ability—and takes for granted some vital ideas about human nature.

Those ideas about human nature are everywhere, they are profoundly important, and the Bible teaches that they are deeply wrong. Let me explain.

My way: the wrong way!

Remember how the song goes: we may make mistakes, have a few regrets, but actually we can do the right thing, if we have the will. That's the first thing the song takes for granted, that we can all choose to do the right thing if we want, although it may be tough.

The second thing the song takes for granted is that we know what the right thing is. Remember the words 'going to hell for a heavenly cause'? That assumes we can recognise a heavenly cause. But that's not obvious. During the twentieth century people did all kinds of things, whether in Nazi Germany, Stalin's Russia or Pol Pot's Cambodia, for what they thought was a heavenly cause, although the judgement of history is that these causes were hellish, not heavenly.

Choose the right?

So that song takes for granted two big things about human nature. First, about our wills, that we can choose to do the right thing. Secondly, about our knowledge, that we can, by ourselves, tell the difference between right and wrong.

Those two assumptions make a huge difference to how you think about spiritual things and salvation. If our wills really can choose to do the right thing, then humans can, in fact, keep God's laws completely. In principle, all by ourselves we can put ourselves straight by sheer will power.

During the history of the Christian church, people have sometimes said something similar; notably, a British monk named Pelagius in the early fifth century. His ideas, often called Pelagianism, were judged wrong by the Council of Carthage in 418. There again, if our knowledge of spiritual things is perfectly competent by itself, then the Bible is not necessary to tell us about God and His will: we can discover it by ourselves.

Know the wrong?

Again, Christians down the years have seen that our knowledge is not intact or competent enough to do this. Orthodox Christian theologians often summed up their misgivings about these two wrong ideas about our wills and knowledge by saying that neither recognises the truth of total depravity.

Clearing the ground

Let's clear away some misunderstandings about total depravity. First, total depravity is not saying that God first created human beings as bad or evil (Genesis 1 v 31 teaches that what God created was good). Total depravity describes human nature after the fall described in Genesis 3—not human nature before it.

Secondly, total depravity isn't saying that humans are as bad as they possibly could be or that all human actions are completely evil.

One of the few things I can cook is a brown beef stew, which I think tastes best with some chilli powder added. The stew isn't completely made of chillies, but the whole stew is permeated with the taste of it. Similarly, total depravity describes how our whole nature is affected by sin. The word 'total' in 'total depravity' is talking about totality in extent: no zone or part of us is untouched by sin.

Thirdly, it's tempting to write off total depravity as 'too bleak', or 'too pessimistic', but of course we're concerned with whether the Bible teaches this, not whether we like it.

Fourthly, only Jesus did not have total depravity. The rest of us do (Romans 3 v 9-18). He, though, is completely human, and was tempted by sin as we are, but, unlike us, did not sin (Hebrews 4 v 15).

Getting it clear

Romans 1 v 18-32 is a good starting point for understanding the biblical idea of total depravity. Paul has described his eagerness to preach the gospel (v 15), explaining that in the gospel is God's power to save (v 16), since it reveals how God sets people right with himself (v 17). Obviously, if the gospel is to do with God setting people right with Himself, that means something was wrong between God and human beings in the first place.

Verses 18-32 spell that wrongness out. God is angry at human actions which suppress the truth (v 18). After all, vital truths about God, His power and divine nature, can be seen from what He has created. But rather than worship God properly, men and women prefer to worship other things, making up gods as they see fit (v 20-23). In this, human thinking becomes 'futile' (v 21). Of course, it's bound to be futile, since humans naturally suppress truth about God rather than embrace it.

Wrong thinking

So here Paul directly picks up human intellectual abilities, what we know. He is not talking about all areas of knowledge—we still know and discover things about the created world around us. But knowledge of our Creator and His will is now futile. That's where our abilities have been impaired. This means that sin affects our knowledge of spiritual things. Part of the 'total' of total depravity is that sin touches and impacts our spiritual understanding.

That means we cannot rely simply on our own understanding to work out what pleases God and what does not. One consequence of total depravity, then, is that we need God to reveal to us who He is and what He wants, because we cannot work that out on our own. That's why the Bible stresses that Jesus does reveal God to us (eg: John 1 v 18, 3 v 13) and that we need, not just to study or even just respect the Bible God has given us, but actually obey it. Total depravity means we need the Bible, because it is God's words to us.

Since total depravity impacts our thinking about spiritual things, we can't seriously think the Bible is wrong and we are right. For men especially in today's world this affects issues of sex ('How can the Bible be so strait-laced about a bit of fun?'), work ('Surely I can do what it takes to get on?') and family ('Do I really have to read with the kids rather than watch the game?').

Total depravity also means we sinfully want to prefer our words or other people's to the Bible's. This temptation will not disappear, because part and parcel of human sinfulness is wanting to defy God and His law (see Romans 1 v 32—we approve of those who do wrong). This temptation will persist in our churches (see 2 Timothy 4 v 1-4, especially v 3), so we must be self-aware about our tendencies as groups, as well as individuals, to rationalise disobeying or marginalising the Bible. That's not our wisdom speaking, but our total depravity.

Wrong choices

That takes us to total depravity and our wills. Can't we just will the right things? We've already mentioned Romans 1 v 32, with its statement that we prefer and approve of, things that displease God. Ephesians 2 v 3 resumes that theme of preferences. Here Paul again describes our state in sin. We are 'dead' in it (v 1). Of course, dead people can do nothing by themselves, and Paul uses that picture of death to remind us we are helpless in our sin.

After all, we have the pressures of the world as well as the oppressive power of Satan bearing down on us (v 2). But there is something else: we live according to our desires and pleasures. Our own preferences are that we actually want to follow the world, or the will of Satan. We rightly talk of sin as slavery (John 8 v 34), but we are willing slaves. Our wills also are touched with sin, so that we prefer sin to righteousness.

So total depravity includes my sinful will. That means that I will not be able to keep God's law entirely by myself, as the Pelagians thought. I have a will, but it is kinked to evil, not neutral, and certainly not good. Since I cannot keep God's law by myself, I cannot earn righteousness or peace with God by my efforts. I can't even make a part payment.

But this preference for evil leaves us not just helplessly bound, but also guilty—justly liable to God's wrath and punishment (Ephesians 2 v 3). Total depravity refers to our helplessness and also our guilt. It therefore means that I need a Saviour, untouched by sins, but who can still justly deal with them. That Saviour is Jesus.

My way or God's way?

Denying total depravity denies the need for Jesus as Saviour. The doctrine of total depravity, therefore, underlines the depth of our need:

- It tells us we need Jesus to reveal God, because sin has corrupted our minds.

- It tells us we need a Saviour, because sin has corrupted our hearts and wills and rendered us guilty.
- It tells us reconciliation with God must be by God's grace, not our merit.

And that also tells us something about why total depravity seems so obnoxious to normal human beings: it knocks our pride. It tells us: we simply can't do it our way.

AUGUSTINE 354-430

The depravity of sin

The first man was unlike us—for a while. Adam was free not to sin. Indeed, he was able to live a sinless life. But he chose otherwise. And we live with the consequences. Which of us can now lead a sinless life? When Adam fell - turning his back on his Maker by eating the forbidden fruit—he dragged us down with him. Like Adam, we proudly crave being our own master. All humanity has followed in his footsteps: so it is now impossible for a man not to sin. Indeed, we are born rebels, because we share Adam's fallen nature. 'Surely I was sinful,' said King David, 'at birth' (Psalm 51 v 5).

This gloomy but sober analysis of humanity's plight was made by the great Christian teacher Augustine—the 'Father of the Western Church'— around 400AD. As the Roman Empire crumbled, Augustine's description of human nature drew on the Bible to oppose the fashionable teaching of Pelagius. British-born, but living in Rome, Pelagius disagreed with Augustine's pessimistic view of human nature, and argued that in principle a man could save himself by moral effort. Jesus was the proof it could be done. He managed to live a sinless life, and therefore, in theory, so can we. Salvation, in other words, is a question of the human will.

'Not so,' replied Augustine, who was Bishop of Hippo in north Africa. Because of Adam, we cannot escape our sinful condition by our own effort. Free will is exercised—we are morally responsible—but we never choose what we should. The reason is that we are no longer free to avoid sin—we are willing sinners, and members of a condemned race. We are biased towards wrong.

'Without God's help, we cannot by free will overcome the temptations of this life.'

So self-help salvation is impossible. Instead, we must depend on God's grace. What rescues and changes men is not human moral effort, but His gift of grace. Augustine—who experienced God's grace in a dramatic conversion—argued that as a result Christians experience delivery from sin in two stages.

In this world, we are able, by God's grace, not to sin. In the next, the ability to sin will be removed: we will be unable to sin at all. It is grace that restores true freedom, in which free will can be exercised to please God.

Peter Ackroyd

'I COULDN'T SLEEP'

Before he became a Christian, Simon didn't care about anything.

'From my late teens through to student life, and then into my twenties, I would do anything to get drunk, stoned, be unpleasant to people (because it was funny), foul-mouthed and a vandal. In quiet moments, I was vaguely aware that I was living in an undesirable way, but that feeling never lasted very long. But strangely, had you challenged me, I would have said that I was quite a decent bloke.'

One day Simon went to a local church with his then girlfriend. As he sat under the Bible's teaching over the space of the following year, he began to understand the truth of the gospel, and its implications for him.

'At the latter stage of that year, I started to realise how completely horrible I was deep down. During the day, I could handle it, because there were lots of things to distract me. But at night, I lay awake acutely aware of my sin and guilt. I dredged up my past, again and again, and was disgusted by it. I knew I was guilty before God, and knew God would judge me for it, and I was terrified.

'After maybe two whole weeks of sleeplessness, I called a Christian friend, and asked for help. It was as he assured me that the promise of God's forgiveness was real that I took hold of it. I walked into his room burdened with guilt, but left with a deep sense of security—knowing that God had forgiven even me.'

BIBLE STUDY

Read Romans 1 v 18-32

Q1. Many people think that sin is 'doing naughty things' that are actually quite pleasurable. What are the hallmarks of sin, according to this passage?

Q2. How would you answer the person who says:
    ★ 'I couldn't help it—I just fell into sin'?
    ★ 'Sinning means we are free'?

Q3. Paul makes the point that the root of sin is that we suppress the knowledge of God our Creator.
    Why does Paul include sexual sin in this passage: What truth about God are people suppressing?

Q4. Why does Paul include such a long list of 'sins' in 29-31? What is curious about the list? How many do you think that you are guilty of?

Q5. How do people normally think that God views our sin? How does this passage correct that thinking?

Q6. How would you respond to these statements?
    ★ The main problem with sin is that it messes up our lives.
    ★ In response to this passage, we should stop sinning and live better lives.

Q7. What implications does this passage have for the way we go about evangelism?

DISCUSS

Q1. 'I've got my faults, but I'm not a bad bloke deep down.' In your experience, is this the way most people think?

Q2. How did you come to the realisation that you were a sinner in God's sight?

Q3. Think of some ways in which we can help people to see that our natures are deeply corrupted. How, in practice, might we talk about these things with men?

Q4. Many people would consider this as a very depressing doctrine, which will lead people into having a 'poor self image.' Why is it actually a liberating truth?

SING TRUTH

God made me for himself,
to serve him here
with love's pure service
and in filial fear
to show his praise,
to labour for him now,
then see his glory
where the angels bow.

All needed grace was mine
through his dear Son
Whose life and death
my full salvation won;
grace that would give me strength
and hold me fast
grace that would seal
and crown my work at last.

And I, poor sinner,
threw it all away,
lived for the work
or pleasure of each day –
as if no Christ had shed
his precious blood,
as if I owed no homage
to my God.

O Holy Spirit,
with your fire divine
melt into tears
this thankless heart of mine:
teach me to love what once
I seemed to hate
and live to God
before it is too late.

H W Baker (1821-1877)

"IN MY PLACE CONDEMNED HE STOOD"

The penal substitution of Christ

Bob Horn

T he world's great religious leaders are all remembered for their life, example and teaching. We remember Jesus for those things too, not least because He lived the only perfect life in all history.

But, astonishingly, Jesus wanted to be remembered chiefly for His death. He repeatedly stressed this in his teaching: 'I am the good shepherd ... I lay down my life for the sheep' 'Greater love has no-one than this, that someone lays down his life for his friends' 'For even the Son of Man came) ... to give his life as a ransom for many'. (John 10 v 14-15; 15 v 13; Mark 10 v 45) Moreover, His four biographies give a full third of their space to the events surrounding His death. To Paul it was 'of first importance ... that Christ died for our sins in accordance with the Scriptures' (1 Corinthians 15 v 3).

Life and resurrection
When Jesus and Paul emphasise Jesus' death, they do not downplay His life or sideline His resurrection. His death is never isolat-

ed from the whole of His coming and triumph. Before He died He claimed that: 'I have authority to take [my life] up again' (John 10 v 18). When Paul asserts that 'Christ died for our sins', he immediately adds as also of first importance that He 'was raised on the third day' (1 Corinthians 15 v 4). Christ's sinless life of obedience and His victorious resurrection are integral to God's rescue plan. Yet it is His death that needs explaining. His resurrection was sensational and unprecedented, but actually not surprising. After all, as Peter said: 'it was not possible for him to be held by [death]' (Acts 2 v 24) and He enjoyed 'the power of an indestructible life' (Hebrews 7 v 16).

Death chosen

History's religious leaders died because death comes to all mortals. Jesus, the God-man, was not subject to death: 'No one takes [my life] from me, but I lay it down of my own accord' (John 10 v 18). He alone chose to die. Why?

- ★ Was it to show us how to face unjust suffering? Yes. 'Christ ... suffered for you, leaving you an example' (1 Peter 2 v 21).
- ★ Was it to show God identifying with us in suffering? Yes. Jesus was 'made in the likeness of men' and 'was numbered with the transgressors' (Philippians 2 v 7; Isaiah 53 v 13).
- ★ Was it to demonstrate the greatness of God's love? Yes. But in becoming flesh, He showed us all those truths; it did not require His death to prove them.

So why did He need to die? Two questions must be faced. First, what outcome was it that only His death could secure? That is, what did His death achieve? Second, how did His death achieve that outcome? These are central questions in the Christian faith; all human destiny depends on the answers to them.

What did the cross achieve?

The Bible describes what the cross achieved using some vivid word pictures:

★ RELATIONSHIPS: The first word pictures the sphere of relationships: reconciliation. Our lifestyle of choice kept God out, but His death brought us a new relationship with God. 'We were reconciled to God by the death of his Son' (Romans 5 v 10).

★ SLAVERY: A second term comes from the realm of slaves or prisoners: redemption. His death gave us freedom and pardon, releasing us from the sentence and curse of sin. 'Christ redeemed us from the curse of the law by becoming a curse for us' (Galatians 3 v 13). 'In him we have redemption through his blood, the forgiveness of our trespasses' (Ephesians 1 v 7).

★ WARFARE: A third term, victory, conjures up a battlefield. We were defeated by sin, losing the struggle against evil and subject to death. But Jesus 'disarmed the powers and authorities ... triumphing over them by the cross' (Colossians 2 v 15:NIV). This points to the wider effects of the cross throughout the cosmos. So 'Thanks be to God, who gives us the victory through our Lord Jesus Christ' (1 Corinthians 15 v 57).

These terms tell us the objective outcomes of the cross; other words tell us how Christ's death applies in our experience.

★ THE LAW COURT: Justification is a word from a court of law, where a judge either condemns or acquits. Because 'God presented Jesus as a sacrifice of atonement' he 'justifies those who have faith in Jesus'. That is, he declares that they may go free, rejoicing in peace, access and hope, never again to face condemnation (Romans 3 v 25-26; see also 5 v 1-2).

★ THE FAMILY: Another such idea comes from the family: adoption. When God justifies sinners on the basis of His Son's death, that clears the way to adopt them as His sons and daughters.

'He predestined us to be adopted as his children through Jesus Christ' (Ephesians 1 v 5:NIV).

These are the great and eternal benefits that the cross achieved. Jesus' incarnation, life and example did not in themselves secure them; they come to us only because He died and rose. That leads us to the second big question:

How did the cross achieve all this?

As we have seen, the cross totally altered the state of affairs between God and us. But how did the cross achieve these outcomes? At least two explanations have been offered.

★ IN HERE: The first suggests that the problem is in here—in us, in our attitude and motivation. What the cross did was to have an effect on us. We are self-centred and self-absorbed; but when we look at the cross, we are moved by the lengths to which God went in His love for us. That changes us on the inside and so now God can forgive and receive us.

★ OUT THERE: The second suggests that the problem was out there. It was in the 'rulers ... the authorities ... the cosmic powers over this present darkness ... the spiritual forces of evil in the heavenly places' (Ephesians 6 v 12). What the cross did was to overcome all the hostile and evil forces in the universe, and thus release us from their power and enable us to relate to God.

★ IN GOD HIMSELF: Both those explanations contain truths, but not the fundamental meaning of the cross. 'When I survey the wondrous cross', it does move me. And I rejoice in the victory Christ has won over evil. But even when the cross moves me, I am still a sinner with a record of offending God. Even though Christ has conquered the powers of darkness, I am still guilty and unfit to enter heaven. I can give no irrefutable answer as to why God should accept me. So the central problem is not in us or out there, but in God Himself, who is holy love.

His just nature profoundly loves holiness and has a deep revulsion against evil; He loves all that is good and is vigorously against all that is evil. So the Bible asserts that 'the wrath of God is revealed from heaven against all ungodliness and unrighteousness of men' (Romans 1 v 18), for we have to say with the psalm: 'Against you, you only, have I sinned' (Psalm 51 v 4).

The central problem is this: how can this God maintain His just character and at the same time welcome the unjust? How can the God of unapproachable light welcome us who walk in darkness without condoning our sin? Or judge us without condemning us? How can His wrath and His mercy meet?

Wrath meets mercy

The answer to these profound questions is that, in the cross, God fully expressed both His wrath and His mercy. In that one moment He fully demonstrated both His justice and His love. The simplest statement of this is: 'Christ died for our sins' (1 Corinthians 15 v 3).

The Bible expands on this in various ways. 'Christ died for sins once for all, the righteous for the unrighteous, to bring you to God' (1 Peter 3 v 18:NIV). He, the innocent and blameless, took what was coming to us. He 'bore our sins in his body' (1 Peter 2 v 24); He carried the penalty that should have landed on us. 'God presented him as a sacrifice of atonement' or 'propitiation'—that is, 'as the one who would turn aside [God's] wrath, taking away our sin' (Romans 3 v 25:NIV—see footnote). He stood in for us, He took our place under God's wrath; we should have been forsaken by His Father, but He took that experience instead of us. He changed places with us—the righteous for the unrighteous. He made Himself our penalty-bearing Substitute.

The Servant, the Son

Isaiah 53 is full of references to Christ, the Servant of the Lord, taking our place. He was 'pierced for our transgressions, he was crushed for our iniquities; the punishment that brought us peace was on him ... the LORD has laid on him the iniquity of us all ... for the transgression of my people he was stricken ... he bore the sin of many' (Isaiah 53 v 5-12:NIV). The constant refrain is crystal clear: He is for us; He went to death instead of us; He showed His love in giving Himself to endure the wrath of God so that, with our penalty paid, we can now be accepted.

God in Christ

'In Christ God was reconciling the world to himself' (2 Corinthians 5 v 19). That was it—'God in Christ'. It was not Christ over against His Father, persuading the unwilling. It was not the Father over against His victim Son, punishing the innocent. It was not God making a third party suffer. It was Father, Son and Spirit acting in total harmony in Their eternal saving plan. 'God so loved ... that he gave his only Son; The Son of God ... gave himself...' (John 3 v 16; Galatians 2 v 20). It was 'through the eternal Spirit' that Christ offered himself (Hebrews 9 v 14). The Trinity were totally at one in what John Stott calls 'the self-substitution of God' on the cross for our salvation.

Only because

It is only because Jesus took our place that the undeserved benefits of reconciliation, redemption and victory have come to us. It is only because He went to the cross that justification and adoption have become ours. We could never have been reconciled if He had not borne our sins; never redeemed had He not paid our penalty; never released had He not triumphed. We could never have been acquitted had He not borne our condemnation; never adopted had He not been forsaken by His Father for us. Christ, our penalty-bearing Substitute, secures the whole scheme of salvation.

Because what Christ did on the cross was a once-for-all, completed work, it gives us security on two fronts. If God were to ask why He should admit us to His heaven, or the devil to point to our guilt and unworthiness, we have one answer: 'Don't look at me—I know I'm sinful and guilty—but look at Jesus, He carried my guilt and paid my penalty'. Neither God nor the devil can resist that answer. That is what Christ's cross achieved; and that is why it is so compelling in our lives.

Compelling

The cross compels those who do not yet know Christ to consider where they stand before God's judgment and before such sacrificial love. And for those who do know Him, 'Christ's love compels us, because we are convinced that one died for all' (2 Corinthians 5 v 14:NIV). It is our great motivator; it stirs us not because we feel some emotional pull, but precisely because we grasp that on the cross Christ died for others, that 'in my place condemned He stood'. Understanding God's explanation of the cross is not abstract theorising; it radically motivates our whole life.

SING TRUTH

Before the throne of God above
I have a strong, a perfect plea,
A great high priest, whose name is love,
Who ever lives and pleads for me.
My name is written on his hands,
My name is hidden in his heart;
I know that while in heaven he stands
No power can force me to depart.

When Satan tempts me to despair
And tells me of the guilt within,
I look to heaven, and see him there
who made an end of all my sin.

Because the sinless Saviour died
My sinful soul is counted free,
For God, the just, is satisfied
To look on him and pardon me.
Behold him there! The risen Lamb,
My perfect, spotless righteousness,
The great unchangeable I AM,
The king of glory and of grace!
One with himself, I cannot die,
My soul is purchased by his blood;
My life is safe with Christ on high,
With Christ, my Saviour and my God.

Charitie L. Bancroft (1841-1923)

'HE DIED IN MY PLACE!'

John Bunyan's timeless classic, Pilgrim's Progress, is, in many ways, autobiographical. He describes it as a 'dream' and says he saw Christian crying out: 'O! My dear wife ... I am in myself undone, by reason of a burden that lieth hard upon me. Moreover, I am for certain informed, that our city will be burnt with fire from heaven ... Except a way of escape be found, whereby we may be delivered.'

Later Christian is told: 'As to your burden, be content to bear it, until you come to the place of deliverance; for there it will fall from your back by itself.'

Bunyan's story continues: 'Up the hill did burdened Christian run, but not without great difficulty, because of the load on his back. He ran until he came to a place somewhat ascending, and upon that place stood a Cross, and a little further, at the bottom, a Sepulchre. So I saw in my dream, that just as Christian came up to the Cross, the Burden loosed from off his shoulders, and fell from his back, and began to tumble, and so continued to do, till it came to the mouth of the Sepulchre, where it fell in, and I saw it no more.

'Then Christian said, with a glad heart, "He has given me rest by his sorrow, and life by his death".'

BIBLE STUDY

Read Isaiah 52 v 13 – 53 v 12

This is the passage from which Philip told the Ethiopian court official 'the good news about Jesus' (Acts 8 v 35).

Q1. How does this passage describe our condition?

Q2. What did it cost Jesus to go to the cross? Make a list of all the things in this passage that Jesus, as God's Servant, did or endured for us.

Q3. What did His dying achieve for us? His death looked like the pointlessly tragic death of an innocent man, so make a list of the benefits that come to us through what He suffered.

Q4. What outcomes from His suffering does this passage predict (v 10-12)?

DISCUSS

Q1. What kind of answers do you come across most to the question: 'Why did Jesus die'?

Q2. How could you use those common notions to explain the real meaning of Jesus' death?

Q3. What aspect of the death of Jesus has struck you most from this chapter—why?

Q4. Understanding the cross should radically move our whole lives in a different direction. How? Be specific and practical!

4

"HOW DO I GET RIGHT WITH GOD?"

Justification by faith alone

Garry Williams

Many people still regard a good life, attendance at church, baptism or confirmation, or more simply, 'just doing your best' as the way to God. How wrong could they be...

Justification is a very important doctrine, both in the history of the church, and in the Bible. The reformer Martin Luther said that right thinking on justification would see the church flourish; wrong thinking would see it perish. For the apostle Paul, wrong teaching on justification was enough to provoke him to oppose in public his fellow apostle Peter (Galatians 2 v 11ff.). He even declared that anyone— even an angel—teaching against the doctrine would be eternally condemned (Galatians 1 v 8).

Our natural plight

To understand this crucial doctrine, picture a man who has committed an appalling series of crimes. There is no doubt of his guilt. In his more self-aware moments he might even admit that he has long been suffering because of his own evil. He has been trapped by his corruption, he has been powerless to escape, he has found himself committing the crimes again and again and again, caught up into a terrible spiral of destruction to himself and others. He knows that he will one day be caught; his conviction and his sentence are sure and certain.

Imagine the cloud which hangs over him. He knows that his punishment, when it comes, will have no end point—it will endure to the end of his life. For this man, there will be no remission for good behaviour, no early release.

This man's condition is the condition of every human being, according to the Bible. Apart from Christ, you and I are this criminal—and worse. We are going to be called, not before a mere human judge in a human courtroom, but before the throne of the holy God Himself (Matthew 25; Romans 2 v 1-16). We will be sentenced not for a fixed span of time until we die, but for endless ages (Mark 9 v 42-50; Revelation 20 v 7-15). We have sinned against an infinitely good God, and the punishment for such sin is infinite. That is our natural plight.

Declared innocent

Now what would it mean for our criminal to be 'justified'? It would mean that, prior to his being brought before the judge, he would be declared innocent of the crimes which he has undoubtedly committed. It would mean that his criminal record would be erased. It would mean that he would be given a promise, now, even prior to the day of his trial, that he will never be punished for the crimes which he has committed. Knowing himself to be the worst of criminals, he would also know himself to be free from all the consequences of all the heinous evil that he has done.

This is the picture which the Bible uses when it speaks of the justification of a Christian believer. It uses language and concepts which take us to such a picture of the judge and the courtroom. When it speaks of Christians being 'justified', it tells us that we are justified now. Before we even come to the Day of Judgment and the courtroom where Christ sits as judge, our justification has been accomplished. Hence Paul can write with confidence that:

'There is therefore now no condemnation for those who are in Christ Jesus' (Romans 8 v 1). He can ask: 'Who can undo the sentence which God has pronounced?' 'Who shall bring any charge against God's elect? It is God who justifies. Who is to condemn?' (Romans 8 v 33-34).

The Bible speaks of people who have turned away from God, and who have thus committed the highest evil, being declared here and now, entirely innocent; being told that they have been acquitted, that they have been vindicated by the Judge Himself. To be justified is to be declared innocent before the throne of the holy God even before you get there.

How can this be?

In particular, how can this be done by a holy and perfect Judge? How will a Judge whose judgments are always based on the truth, declare sinful men innocent? How can the God who said: 'Acquitting the guilty and condemning the innocent—the LORD detests them both' (Proverbs 17 v 15:NIV) seemingly do this very thing? How can the Lord be faithful to the terms of His own covenant, which require punishing those who break it (Leviticus 26 v 14-45) and at the same time be faithful to His promise to bless a great nation from Abraham (Genesis 12 v 1-3)? The answer to this question lies in understanding what it means to be justified by faith.

Real faith: know, agree, trust

Faith in the Bible has three elements. First of all, we need to know the thing in which we believe. This is obvious: I can only believe in Jesus Christ if I know about Him. Faith involves mental knowledge. But this is not enough by itself, since I must not only know about the gospel, I must also agree with it. I might, for example, know that it is claimed that Brazil has the greatest soccer team in the world, but hold the opinion that England is better. I can know without agreeing. Real faith is knowing and agreeing.

But even that is not enough by itself. Think of the demons—as James reminds us in his letter, they believe that there is one God (see James 2 v 19). When we read that they believe that there is one God, this means that they know and agree that the great Israelite confession of Deuteronomy is true: 'Hear O Israel: The LORD our God, the LORD is one' (Deuteronomy 6 v 4). The demons believe the creed of Israel! But obviously they do not have a saving faith in God. What is lacking?

The third element of faith—trust. The demons do not trust in Jesus Christ as their Saviour. So someone can know and agree, but not trust. I have even met non-Christians who say that this is true of them: they know the gospel, they think it is true, but they will not trust in Jesus Christ as their own Saviour and Lord. That is a terrifying thing. It is not faith, because it does not involve personal trust.

Real faith: a bridge

Now back to our question: how can the just Judge declare the guilty to be innocent? Martin Luther explained that faith is not just about mental assent; it is about a particular personal relationship to Jesus Christ:

> 'The third incomparable benefit of faith is that it unites the soul with Christ as a bride is united with her bridegroom. By this mystery, as the Apostle teaches, Christ and the soul become one flesh [a reference to Ephesians 5 v 31-32]. And if they are one flesh and there is between them a true marriage—indeed the most perfect of all marriages … —it follows that everything they have, they hold in common, the good as well as the evil. Accordingly, the believing soul can boast of, and glory in, whatever Christ has as though it were its own, and whatever the soul has Christ claims as his own. Let us compare these and we shall see inestimable benefits. Christ is full of grace, life and salvation. The soul is full of sins, death and damnation. Now let faith come between them and sins, death and damnation will be Christ's, while grace, life and salvation will be the soul's.'

> Three Treatises [Philadelphia: Fortress, 1970] p. 286

Do you see Luther's point? He is saying that when we believe in Jesus Christ we are one with Him. The Holy Spirit unites us, by faith, with Jesus. Faith therefore acts like a bridge, a bridge which my sin crosses to Christ and across which His righteousness comes to me.

Real faith: uniting to Christ

Of course, Luther knew this because he read Paul. Paul explains that when we are baptised we are 'clothed' with Christ: 'All of you who were baptised into Christ have clothed yourselves with Christ' (Galatians 3 v 27). Indeed, he explains that it is being clothed with Christ which makes us sons of God (3 v 26).

In other words, becoming a Christian and being baptised into Christ clothes us with Christ, which gives us a new status as sons of God. Hence, by being united to Christ in His life, death, and resurrection, we are clothed in Him, we become what He is. He is the Son of God, and we become sons of God in Him.

By being united to Him, we become righteous as He is righteous. We share in His righteousness. No wonder then that in Philippians 3 v 9 Paul speaks of having a righteousness 'which comes through faith in Christ, the righteousness from God that depends on faith'. Faith unites us to Christ so that all that He is becomes ours, and all that we are becomes His. What a wonderful exchange!

Real faith: rich in Christ

This is why the just Judge can declare guilty sinners righteous. Guilty sinners can be declared righteous because they are righteous, in Christ! Their guilt and punishment have gone from them, have been taken by Jesus, who died in their place bearing their guilt and punishment on the cross (Romans 3 v 25; 8 v 3; 2 Corinthians 5 v 21; Galatians 3 v 13). What love to take from us such sin and suffering!

And His flawless righteousness has come to sinners, has been given to them by faith. All that He is, we are. If He is perfectly innocent, we are perfectly innocent. And was Jesus innocent? Some thought not—they thought Him cursed for His own sins because He had died on a tree (Deuteronomy 21 v 22-23). But God declared Jesus to be innocent when He raised Him from the dead. He declared that Jesus had not died for His own sins, but in the place of others for their sins.

In His resurrection from the dead, Jesus Christ was vindicated (literally 'justified') by God's Spirit (1 Timothy 3 v 16). And if Jesus has been declared innocent, we are declared innocent when we are clothed with Him. The believing soul can truly claim whatever Christ has as its own. This is no legal game of 'let's pretend'. The believer is united to Jesus, so that what is Christ's is indeed the believer's. What riches we receive!

Real faith: a gift from God

How do we get this faith by which we are justified? Do we screw up our eyes and try harder to believe in Jesus? Do we search deep within the darkness of our souls for the grain of faith which lies concealed there? Do we seek to set aside the business of our lives to find faith in the silence?

No—faith is not something which comes from within us.

Few comments can be more frustrating for the Christian from a non-Christian friend than 'I wish I had your faith'. If someone wishes to have faith, if they really, sincerely wish to have it, they have simply to ask for it. God gives faith as a gift. It is not a good work which we do. It is something which He bestows on us in His generosity: 'By grace you have been saved through faith. And this is not your own doing; it is the gift of God, not a result of works, so that no one may boast.' (Ephesians 2 v 8-9) The Christian can rejoice in his justification, but he can never boast in it as if it were his own doing. It is the sovereign gift of God.

What then?

And what does our criminal do after he has been told in advance that he will be acquitted when his day of trial comes? Does he decide to press on in his life of crime? Does the justified sinner go on sinning with abandon, thinking that he is free from punishment, thinking that he can make God even more generous by notching up even more sin for him to forgive (Romans 6 v 1)? No, he does not, and for many reasons.

First and foremost, because justification by faith is not an isolated thing. It comes with the other great works of God in the soul described elsewhere in this book. For example, a justified soul is also a regenerated soul, which means that it is a renewed soul. And a renewed soul is not one that will go on sinning as it did in its old state. As it is often put, faith alone justifies, but the faith which justifies is never alone: it is always accompanied by moral change and renewal.

This is why the Bible so often speaks of the last judgment being a judgment based on testing our works. How can this be if we are justified by faith alone? Because the genuineness of our faith will be demonstrated by our works. Hence Jesus can speak of someone who cares for a Christian being justified (Matthew 25 v 31-46), because the behaviour reveals that the person truly loves and trusts in Jesus Himself. The fruit of the tree shows what kind of tree it is (Matthew 7 v 15-20).

We are justified by faith alone; it is the glorious freedom of the believer, freedom from the futile attempt to do the impossible, to scrub out the foulness of our guilt by ourselves. It is freedom from guilt, and freedom from punishment, but it is not freedom to sin!

MARTIN LUTHER
1583 – 1546

Justified!

The Reformation of the 16th century changed the face of human history. It changed politics, education, art, music, and literature. But most of all it brought the light of the gospel to Europe.

At its heart was the gospel of justification by faith alone, discovered in the pages of Scripture by Martin Luther. Luther was a monk, raised on a rich diet of Roman Catholic theology. He had been taught that he would be saved by doing his best, by striving with every fibre of his natural being to do what was in him. Although this would not actually be enough to please God, God would graciously consider it to be enough. In the exam of life, Luther at his best might only make, say, 40%, but his teachers told him that God would reckon this to be enough for his justification, to be 100%.

For Luther, even such a reduced pass mark was too much. How could he ever know that he had done even his own best? As he put it: 'I lived an irreproachable life as a monk'. He toiled and laboured for his justification, but it always eluded him. He found sin at large within himself and he doubted the sincerity and sufficiency of his own confession. He came even to hate God for His righteousness.

Until, that is, he discovered, in the Psalms and in Paul, that God's righteousness is not just the righteousness by which He judges, but also the righteousness which in His mercy He gives to His people to make them right. That discovery sparked a change in Luther's life, and as he made it public, it sparked the tinders of Europe, and of the world.

'NOT "PLEASE", BUT "THANK YOU"'

Steve was raised in a family where there was a strong sense of duty about going to church. But there was never any reality about it, only a growing sense of resentment...

'Before I became a Christian, I thought living God's way was all about trying to win God's favour. I thought it was about saying 'please' to God: "Please save me".

'But once I understood the gospel, I had to turn my thinking upside down. I couldn't earn God's favour. I could only receive it as a gift through Jesus' death for me. I learnt that living God's way is all about responding to God's favour and forgiveness, not a way of earning his acceptance.

'So it's not about saying 'please' to God. It's about saying 'thank you': "Thank you God for saving me through the cross of Jesus". To me, living as a Christian is a life-long thank you for His grace.

'I try to say thank you to God for His grace by living with Jesus as my Lord, encouraging other Christians to live that way, and inviting people who don't know Christ to accept Him as Lord. But I often fail in all these things.

'Thankfully, God continues to be gracious and I throw myself back to the cross and ask once again for God's mercy and forgiveness.'

BIBLE STUDY

Read Romans 4 v 1-12

Paul begins by asking what Abraham discovered 'in this matter' (v 1:NIV). Read back over Chapter 3 and try to summarise what 'this matter' is – what problem has Paul been discussing, and what solution has he found?

He now takes Abraham and David as case-studies of justification by faith alone. Read Genesis 15, 17 v 1-14 and Psalm 32 for the Old Testament background to this passage.

Q1. What exactly did Abraham believe?

Q2. What did David trust in for his hope?

Q3. In v 4-5 Paul explains the difference between a gift and a wage. What is it?

Q4. What kind of people does Paul say that God justifies (v 5)? From the material in this chapter, can you explain how God can do this without doing what He prohibits in Proverbs 17 v 15?

Q5. In v 9 Paul then widens the scope beyond circumcised Jews. How does he prove that justification by faith alone is for the uncircumcised as well as the circumcised?

Q6. What was circumcision all about (v 11)?

Q7. Whose father is Abraham? Why (v 11-12)?

Q8. All of this is a case-study of the doctrine set out in Chapter 3 of Romans. There, Paul's application is that all boasting is excluded (v 27, repeated in 4 v 2). How might you be tempted to boast, and how can you use Romans 4 v 1-12 to train your mind to flee from the temptation to boast?

DISCUSS

Q1. What are some of the things that people today think will keep them 'right with God'?

Q2. Many Christians today try to add works to faith. 'We get to heaven by trusting Jesus and...' What are some of the things that we falsely add to 'faith alone'?

Q3. What would you answer to someone who says: 'I wish I had your faith'?

5 "WHO'S IN CHARGE?"

The sovereignty of God the Father

Liam Goligher

The Bible's declaration that God is in charge of the world seems curiously at odds with the seeming chaos we observe in the world and in our own lives...

'What comes into our minds when we think about God is the most important thing about us' (A. W. Tozer). Yet it is becoming increasingly popular for theologians (including some who insist on calling themselves evangelicals) to think of God as performing without a script. They say that God is in process: that, like the rest of us, He is working things out as He goes along, suffering the fluid circumstances of life in this universe and changing His plans to fit the new situation. But nothing could be more out of step with the revelation of God we find in the Bible.

Ephesians 1 tells us that He 'works all things according to the counsel of his will'. What is included in God's purpose and plan? Our text says 'all things.' You cannot get more comprehensive than that! This teaching asserts the sovereignty of God.

When we speak about sovereignty we are talking about authority and power. As sovereign, God is the supreme authority in heaven and earth. All other forms of authority exist either by God's command or by God's permission. Sovereignty also means that there is nothing God cannot do—He rules with absolute power and wisdom. He determines what is going to happen, and it does happen. God is not alarmed, thwarted, frustrated or defeated by circumstances or by the sin and rebellion of His creatures. The Bible talks about God's sovereignty in the realms of nature and grace.

God is sovereign in the realm of nature

John Calvin wrote much about the world as a theatre in which God's glory is displayed for all to see. 'The heavens declare the glory of God' (Psalm 19 v 1). He delights to display His wisdom and power—so He creates a universe in which the sheer beauty and workmanship tell us about His skill and strength.

He made it

The universe is His creation. He made it out of nothing. Scripture takes us back to eternity past, when God alone existed. 'In the beginning, God...' (Genesis 1 v 1). He alone is totally free and self-sufficient. He does not need humans or anything in all creation (Acts 17 v 25). In short, God is God (Exodus 3 v 14).

Why did God create the universe? Why does God do everything else that He does? God Himself tells us in His word: 'Our God is in the heavens. He does all that he pleases' (Psalm 115 v 3; cf. Daniel 4 v 35). He does as He pleases, always as He pleases, only as He pleases.

The evangelical tradition has always had a high doctrine of creation; this particularly affects our view of humanity. If a cheap piece of pottery falls from the cupboard and smashes, it's not a concern—we just sweep it up and that's that. But if the vase is a priceless antique in a museum, a master's signature edition, and it is destroyed, that is a great tragedy. The difference doesn't lie in the quality of the material (both may have been clay pots), but in the greatness of the artist and the uniqueness of the work.

So too, we humans are not merely spirits caged in the prison-house of a body, but great works of art intended to have a certain enthusiasm and sense of dignity about being human because we are made in the image of God.

He owns it

The universe is His possession. Psalm 24 v 1 declares: 'The earth is the LORD's and the fulness thereof, the world and those who dwell therein'. The prophets call Him 'the God of the whole earth' and say that 'the Most High rules the kingdom of men and gives it to whom he will' (Isaiah 54 v 5; Daniel 4 v 17; 25). The apostle Paul told the Athenians, 'in him we live and move and have our being' (Acts 17 v 28).

One of the implications of this for Christians is that there is no area of life that is outside God's rule. God did not create a separation between the 'secular' and the 'sacred,' as many Christians today often do. Christians are meant to participate alongside non-Christians in every aspect of life. We are to see His 'common grace' in everything that is true and beautiful and lovely. Christians are to permeate society and work for the transformation of the world and its cultures.

He rules it

The universe is His dominion. This God is a 'hands-on' God and His rule is all-pervasive and all-powerful. Even Satan is powerless without God's sovereign permission to act.

The word 'providence' refers to God's good government of our world and of our lives. Christ 'upholds the universe by the word of his power' (Hebrews 1 v 3), and Paul argues that 'in him all things hold together' (Colossians 1 v 17). The Heidelberg Catechism defines providence as:

> 'the almighty and ever present power of God whereby he still upholds, as it were by his own hands, heaven and earth together with all creatures, and rules in such a way that leaves and grass, rain and drought, fruitful and unfruitful years, food and drink, health and sickness, riches and poverty, and everything else, come to us, not by chance but by his fatherly hand' (Question 27).

Proverbs 16 v 1 applies God's rule to human words: 'The plans of the heart belong to man, but the answer of the tongue is from the LORD.'' Proverbs 21 v 1 applies the principle to human affections: 'The king's heart is a stream of water in the hand of the LORD; he turns it wherever he will.' He rules over people's actions: 'Many are the plans in the mind of a man, but it is the purpose of the LORD that will stand' (Proverbs 19 v 21). Believers are encouraged to believe that 'all things work together for good, for those who are called according to his purpose' (Romans 8 v 28).

Without sovereignty God would not be God. If He were subject to any other authority or power, then He would have less power and authority than they had. Even if there was one single molecule in this universe running around loose, totally free of God's sovereignty, then we would have no guarantee that a single promise of God would ever be fulfilled. Maybe this one molecule would wreck the course of God's purposes and even prevent Christ from returning!

God is sovereign in the realm of grace

Evangelical theology takes sin seriously and argues with Paul that believers 'were dead in trespasses and sins' and that 'the unbeliever doesn't understand the things of the Spirit of God; neither can he know them...' (Ephesians 2 v 1-3; 1 Corinthians 2 v 14). It is against this background that we talk about the sovereignty of God's grace. We mean by this that salvation is neither initiated by human choice nor appropriated by human effort; it begins and ends with God.

He chose us

'He chose us in [Christ] before the foundation of the world' (Ephesians 1 v 4-11). Here, as in so many places, the Bible tells us that God had His eye on us long before we had ours on Him. 'Herein is love: not that we loved God, but that He loved us.' I grew up with the illustration: 'God has cast His vote for your soul; Satan cast his, but you must cast the deciding ballot.' This, however, doesn't square with the apostle Paul's remark that: 'It depends not on human will or exertion, but on God, who has mercy' (Romans 9 v 16). Election is not only a prominent doctrine in the Bible, but is of immeasurable comfort to those who are always anxious about whether they are doing enough to secure their salvation. Election teaches us, in Christ's own words: 'You did not choose me, but I chose you and appointed you that you should go and bear fruit and that your fruit should abide' (John 15 v 16).

He saves us

We can say that salvation is by grace alone in Christ alone, through faith alone.

Salvation is by grace alone

When we speak of grace alone (sola gratia), we are speaking of the fact that God saves us, because of His mercy and graciousness toward us, and not because of something—indeed anything—in us that makes us desirable to God. We are sinful, we do not seek God, we do not understand God, we do not obey God's law, and indeed, says Paul, we cannot! (Romans 3 v 10-12).

Jesus says exactly the same thing. 'No one can come to me unless the Father who sent me draws him. And I will raise him up on the last day.' (John 6 v 44) In other words, you cannot come to God unless you are drawn. Jesus went on to say in verse 65: 'This is why I told you that no one can come to me unless it is granted him by the Father'. So unless we are enabled to come to the Father, we cannot and indeed will not turn to God and embrace Jesus Christ.

Our salvation depends upon God's graciousness and not upon our goodness.

Salvation is in Christ alone

Everything that possibly can be done for our salvation is done

JOHN CALVIN
1509 – 1564

John Calvin defended the doctrine of God's exhaustive sovereignty over all things, especially over the salvation and damnation of individual human beings. For some, this makes him an ogre—teaching terrible doctrines which should never be uttered.

That was the case in his own day as much as it is now. Indeed, it was the fact that so many people were attacking the Bible's view of God's sovereignty that provoked Calvin to write in response.

For Calvin, God's sovereignty was not just a truth to be believed in his mind; it was a truth which he lived day by day. Geneva, where he worked, only became a shining beacon of the Reformation by means of a long hard struggle on Calvin's part. He was bitterly opposed by heretics flooding into the city, and by Libertines, old Genevan families who did not like Calvin's insistence on the gospel.

It was Calvin's confidence in the sovereignty of God which enabled him to persevere in his attempts to reform the city, even to the point where he was expelled soon after he arrived. Within a few years his exile in Strasbourg ended as the Genevans invited him back to continue the work. But had the invitation never come, had the Genevan Academy never been founded, had the missionaries who would convert so many in France never been sent, doubtless Calvin would have been content to obey, and to trust God's sovereignty to achieve the purposes of God's kingdom.

Garry Williams

through the birth, life, death and resurrection of our Lord Jesus Christ. The cross was the judgment of God on Christ as the believer's substitute. Christ stood in for us and took the rap that was justly meant for us. But the storm passed and the resurrection of Christ confirmed Him as the King of creation, the Lord of redemption. 'He was crucified for our sins and was raised for our justification' (Romans 4 v 25:NIV). His death accomplished a salvation that is infinite in its value. But He had a particular people on His mind as He went to the cross. We hear Him pray in the upper room: 'I am not praying for the world but for those whom you have given me ... for their sake I consecrate myself' (John 17 v 9, 19).

Salvation is through faith alone

The central doctrine of the Reformation was justification by grace alone through faith alone. We believe that, by trusting in Christ alone for our salvation, we are declared righteous. All of Christ's perfect obedience is charged to our account and our sins are regarded as having been paid for at the cross. We are declared righteous before God in an instant, as the merit of the perfect life and atoning sacrifice of our Lord is credited to our account. What we need is this 'alien' or 'foreign' righteousness; that is, a righteousness that belongs properly to someone else, but is given to us as though it really were our own. Besides the banking image of credit, the Bible uses the image of a white robe that covers our sinfulness and shame.

It was this robe that God used to cover Adam and Eve, when they realised that their fig leaves would not hide them from God's judgment. And it was this covering that was foreshadowed in the sacrifices, until John the Baptist declared, 'Behold, the Lamb of God, who takes away the sin of the world!'

He keeps us

God has promised two blessings of salvation for the elect. First, He has promised to keep them forever, and never to forsake them.

Second, He has promised to work within them so that they will never fall away from Him. Both blessings are expressly promised in Jeremiah 32 v 40: 'I will make with them an everlasting covenant, that I will not turn away from doing good to them. And I will put the fear of me in their hearts, that they may not turn from me'.

Jesus says: 'I give them eternal life, and they will never perish, and no one will snatch them out of my hand' (John 10 v 28-30). It is true that on occasion the elect slip and fall into sin. But when they do, God catches them and makes them stand again (Romans 14 v 4; cf. Deuteronomy 33 v 27). Even when the elect let go of God's hand, God's hand does not let go of them: 'Though he fall, he shall not be cast headlong, for the LORD upholds his hand' (Psalm 37 v 24).

Our response to God's sovereignty

Humility

The doctrines of grace humble the sinner and encourage the saint by giving God His due place. These doctrines also give great glory to God. God is God, and He will not give His glory to another (Isaiah 42 v 8). Reformed theology recognizes that we exist for God's glory.

Confidence

'If God is for us, who can be against us?' (Romans 8 v 31). This doctrine invigorates the believer and motivates our evangelism. It is because God does the work that we can be bold to join Him in it, as He commands us to do. We can do so joyfully, knowing that our efforts will never be in vain.

Worship

'The Lord God the Almighty reigns' (Revelation 19 v 6). God is King over everything that is, was, or ever shall be (Psalm 93 v 1-2; 103 v 19). He is the absolute monarch, the King of kings

(Revelation 19 v 16). This is what we mean by the sovereignty of God. He has total authority over everything. Not only did He decree everything that happens in time, but He sovereignly guides all things by His providence (Romans 8 v 28). He 'works all things according to the counsel of his will' (Ephesians 1 v 11).

'What is the final purpose for which God does all things?' Jonathan Edwards wrote. 'The great end of God's works, which is so variously expressed in Scripture, is indeed one; and this one end is most properly and comprehensively called the glory of God.'

The final goal of the whole universe is the glory of God. 'For from him and through him and to him are all things. To him be glory forever. Amen.' (Romans 11 v 36).

DISCUSS

Q1. If God is not sovereign, what are the implications?

Q2. What is right and what is wrong with the phrase Christians sometimes use: 'Let go and let God'.

Q3. In what particular area of your life is God calling you to trust His sovereignty at present?

BIBLE STUDY

Read Ephesians 1 v 3-14

Q1. What evidence is there from the text of a 'plan' of salvation?

Q2. Can you trace the role of the Trinity in the outworking of the plan of salvation (v 3, 5, 13)?

Q3. What is the scope of the blessings described here (see v 11-14)?

Q4. What is God great purpose in putting this plan into effect (v 5, 6, 9, 14)?

'IF GOD DOES SOMETHING IN YOUR LIFE, WOULD YOU CHANGE IT?'

James Montgomery Boice was a pastor in Philadelphia, USA, for 30 years. On Good Friday 2000, he was diagnosed with a virulent form of cancer. He was to die six weeks later. In his last public address to his congregation he explained his illness, and then added this poignant comment:

> 'If I were to reflect on what goes on theologically here, there are two things I would stress. One is the sovereignty of God. That's not novel. We have talked about the sovereignty of God here forever. God is in charge. When things like this come into our lives, they are not accidental. It's not as if God somehow forgot what was going on, and something bad slipped by.

> 'God does everything according to His will. We've always said that. But what I've been impressed with mostly is something in addition to that. It's possible, isn't it, to conceive of God as sovereign and yet indifferent? God's in charge, but He doesn't care. But it's not that. God is not only the one who is in charge; God is also good. Everything He does is good.

> 'And what Romans 12 v 1 and 2 says is that we have the opportunity by the renewal of our minds—that is, how we think about these things—actually to prove what God's will is. And then it says, "His good, pleasing, and perfect will." Is that good, pleasing, and perfect to God? Yes, of course, but the point of it is that it's good, pleasing, and perfect to us.

> 'If God does something in your life, would you change it? If you'd change it, you'd make it worse. It wouldn't be as good. So that's the way we want to accept it and move forward, and who knows what God will do?'

6 "IS CHANGE POSSIBLE?"

Regeneration by the Holy Spirit

David Field

H ow is it that sinful human beings can be changed so that we are like Christ?

What's the problem?

Why are things not as they should be in the world, and in my life in particular? People answer that question in two different ways.

Many think that things are in such a mess because of what's 'out there'. The environment is the problem, other people are the problem, things that have happened to me or been done to me are the problem. This is the cry of the criminal who pleads: 'Society is to blame!' But, ultimately, that means that the world's mess is God's fault because He is the one who sets the conditions in which we operate.

Others—and they are certainly in a minority—believe that the reason that things are not as they should be in our lives lies 'in here' within ourselves. The problem, as Jesus puts it, is not what enters the body from the outside but the corruption of the human heart. I am a bad tree so I produce bad fruit. I am hostile to God and so I do not submit to His law. (See Matthew 15 v 10-20; 12 v 33-35; Romans 8 v 7-8.)

What's the solution?

These two schools of thought offer radically different solutions to the problem.

If you locate the problems of the human race in what's 'out there', then you take up arms against the wicked external forces that have messed up your life. You'll put your trust in political programmes, new methods of education, economic growth, technological advance, different diets or one of a million other 'saviours', which promise a problem-free and risk-free life while leaving your 'heart' untouched.

On the other hand, if our problem is an inside problem, then the solution can only be found by an inward renewal and deep personal change. It is not that the bad tree needs more sun or fertiliser—all that would do is produce more bad fruit! Rather, its very nature needs changing.

How can this happen?

What is needed is a radical, inward renewal which changes the deepest level of the human person from being self-centred to being God-and-other-person-centred. In order to get rid of sin I 'merely' need to stop being a sinner!

It's obvious that this is beyond the moral endeavours of already sinful human beings. To ask a sinner to bring about deep, inward moral and spiritual change in himself is to ask an Everton fan to join the Kop singing: You'll never walk alone, or—more biblically—the leopard to change his spots or the Ethiopian to change the colour of his skin (Jeremiah 13 v 23). By our natural human instincts, this is what we want to do: to achieve this change ourselves—and yet it is impossible.

The only way that the corruption of a sinner's nature will be dealt with is if God, the Creator-Redeemer, steps in. The God who gave life to human beings in the first place by breathing into dust must breathe a second time by His life-giving Spirit to bring about a new creation, a new human being in Christ (Genesis 2 v 7, John

20 v 21-23; Romans 8 v 9). When it comes to killing germs or refreshing unreached parts, nothing in all creation compares with the uncreated and sovereign Spirit of Almighty God.

What goes on?

The Bible describes this change that God brings about in different ways:

- ★ Joined to Jesus: the sinner is joined by the work of the Spirit to the life of Jesus and so becomes a new creation—John 20 v 21-22; Ephesians 2 v 10; 2 Corinthians 5 v 17.
- ★ Raised: the sinner as corrupt is dead but the Spirit, who is the personal power of the resurrection of Jesus, raises him from the dead—a spiritual resurrection takes place—Ephesians 1 v 18 – 2 v 10; Romans 6 v 1-11; 8 v 1-11.
- ★ Born again: the sinner needs a new heart and a whole new start and by the action of the Spirit, he is granted new birth or birth from above—John 3 v 1-8; 1 Peter 1 v 3, 23; James 1 v 18.

On what basis?

What these images make abundantly clear is this simple fact: the inward renewal and new spiritual start which is regeneration is an act of God's sovereign grace. In other words, it is something that God does for us, not something we achieve by ourselves.

How could what does not exist bring itself into existence? The grace of God is the explanation for the gift of regeneration. And like all the saving grace of God, it is for the sake of, and in union with, the risen Lord Jesus Christ that it happens (1 Peter 1 v 3). It is by bringing us into contact or union with the life of Jesus that the Spirit makes us to share in His resurrection. (See also Romans 6 v 1-11 and 8 v 9-11.)

By what means?

From the creation of the world, God has been doing His work by word and Spirit. And so it is that the regenerating act of God the Holy Spirit, though it is deep, secret, inaccessible, sovereign and gracious, is done by means of the word of God. Just as in the very words 'Stretch out your hand', Jesus communicated healing and strengthening power to the man with the withered arm (Mark 3 v 5), and just as in the very words 'Lazarus, come out', Jesus communicated life to the dead man in the tomb (John 11 v 43), so it is by the life-giving word of the gospel breathed into men by the Spirit, that the spiritually dead are raised and spiritual rebirth happens (James 1 v 18, 1 Peter 1 v 23).

How does it feel?

It is at this point that many people make a simple mistake. Because the images the Bible uses are so dramatic, we make the assumption that the experience of regeneration should also be dramatic, and emotional.

But how did it feel to be born? How did it feel for creation to be created? We don't know these things. Nor is there an experience with its own set of feelings which the Bible labels 'regeneration'. Massive things take place, huge changes are brought about, a person's whole identity is transformed and yet this is a deep work of the Spirit rather than a particularly felt experience of the human subject.

How does it show?

Jesus tells Nicodemus: 'The wind blows where it wishes, and you hear its sound, but you do not know where it comes from or where it goes. So it is with everyone who is born of the Spirit' (John 3 v 8). Although the inward renewal of regeneration is not a felt experience, it certainly leads to a most profound and visible change.

The tree has changed and so the fruit does too. The heart has changed and so too does what comes out of it. The orientation has changed and so too does the direction in which the person is walking.

The first sign is that the person believes the gospel message. It's pointless trying to separate the moment of regeneration from the moment (if there is a 'moment') of repentance and faith, but we should certainly recognise that only by a sovereign renewal of our nature will the person who hated God (Romans 8 v 7), and could not come to Jesus (John 6 v 65), actually repent and believe.

But the new-born human now has a whole new set of attitudes too. His attitude to Christ is utterly different—Christ is now everything to him. His desires and emotions, his perspectives and associations, his hopes and fears and ambitions—all have changed. 'If anyone is in Christ, he is a new creation. The old has passed away; behold, the new has come' (2 Corinthians 5 v 17).

How long does it take?

While the act of regeneration takes place in a moment (although an individual may not be aware of when exactly it happened), the outworking of regeneration lasts a lifetime. This new creation, this new-born person, must grow up and become increasingly true to his transformed core identity as a lover of God.

This will involve putting to death the ways and words which belonged to his dead, old self and yet which are hanging over like the stench left by the previous occupant of a house. And it will involve the deliberate cultivation of the fruit of the Spirit, the graces of the Christian disciple, the evidences that the tree is now good.

Sometimes, therefore, Christian writers have referred to this whole lifelong process of moral and spiritual renewal as regeneration. Usually, however, it is the no-help-needed, Spirit-given, deep-down, by-the-word once-off start of this process, by the recreation and powerful cleansing of the human heart, that is referred to as regeneration.

JOHN OWEN
1616 – 1683

Owen is one of England's theological giants. He lived through the turmoil of the civil war, and was often right in the thick of it. He was a leading advisor to Cromwell and was later the vice-Chancellor of Oxford University.

However, he was primarily a non-conformist pastor and so, when the monarchy was restored, his ministry was restricted and marginalised for a number of years. After the plague and the Great Fire, he ended his life pastoring a London church, publishing and writing. Although much of his writing can seem at first appearance to be rather dense and dry (his collected works run to 23 volumes), it contains pure gold and refreshing water.

Owen did not write for those who are content with a superficial treatment. Rather, his works have manliness and depth and show a concern for precision and thoroughness. Above all, Owen was a man who put truth to work by exploring the 'uses' of doctrine.

This is perhaps best illustrated in his writings about the Christian life. Here we meet Owen the physician who knows exactly how we tick. He skillfully diagnoses the nature, extent and deceitfulness of the believer's indwelling sin and then points out the resources the gospel offers to confront sin head on. At odds with much modern thinking, he offers us no easy steps to victory but instead, he arms and briefs us with a gospel-centred battle plan for a lifelong war with sin in the pursuit of holiness.   **Martyn Cowan**

What does it all mean?

It means everything. It's the difference between being welcomed into the new heavens and new earth (where nothing that defiles is allowed—Revelation 21 v 27), and being sent to hell (where the filth of the universe collects).

It's the difference between being a true and proper human being in union with Jesus Christ, the one true Man, and being a distortion of, and shadow of, a human being. By God's work of regeneration, normal service begins to be resumed in the life of a man. And as for its implications, they tumble over themselves with mind-bending and life-transforming richness. When we understand the Bible's teaching on regeneration...

Implications

★ we understand what is wrong with the world and how to put it right—the human heart is what is wrong and a divine intervention to renew it in union with Jesus Christ is what is needed.

★ we give all praise to God for our salvation, realising that we had as much to do with it as we did with our human birth.

★ we recognise that God is passionately opposed to sin in every way and that the free forgiveness which we receive on the basis of the work of Christ is always accompanied by a deep cleansing of the corruption of the human heart.

★ we delight in the fact that the people of God are 'saints' which means 'those who have been cleaned up so that they have access to the sanctuary' (see Romans 1 v 7, 1 Corinthians 1 v 2).

★ we marvel that, as those who have experienced inward renewal, Christians are fit dwelling-places for God by his Spirit (1 Corinthians 3 v 16; 6 v 19; Ephesians 2 v 21-22; 5 v 18).

★ we see the centrality of the word of God in the accomplishment of His purposes as the means by which He both gives new life to the dead and shapes and cultivates that new life in the Christian disciple (John 6 v 63, 68; Colossians 3 v 16; 2 Timothy 3 v 16-17).

★ we recognise that those who look at the freeness of forgiveness and conclude that God is unconcerned with the state of our hearts and lives could not be more wrong—the people whom God freely forgives are always and exactly the same people whom He radically renews by the Spirit (Romans 6).

★ we acknowledge the Spirit as giver of life and live with a profound dependence on and gratitude to Him (Galatians 5 v 25).

★ on the basis of what has happened to our spirit, we have hope for the renewal of our bodies, and on the basis of what will happen to our bodies, we hope for the regeneration of the universe too (Romans 8 v 11, 20-25; Matthew 19 v 28).

DISCUSS

Q1. What answers do you think most people would give to the question: 'What is wrong with the world'?

Q2. If God changing us is an act of His doing, what is the point in talking about it, since it's beyond our control?

Q3. What would you say to the following?

a) 'The heart of being a Christian is trying to live according to the moral teaching of Jesus.'

b) 'The heart of being a Christian is a deep, invisible, spiritual experience—talk about behaviour is just moralism.'

Q4. How do you tell if you are 'born again'? How do you tell if someone else is truly converted?

BIBLE STUDY

Read James 1 v 1-27

Q1. How and why can troubles be an occasion for rejoicing ? See v 2-4.

Q2. Where and how can you get the ability to 'see things God's way' (= wisdom) ? See v 5-8.

Q3. Explain how 'what's inside', not 'what's outside', counts for most in v 9-12.

Q4. Where do 'sin-babies' (see v 15) not come from, where do they come from, what do they grow into, and how does this affect our attitude to God and to ourselves? See v13-15.

Q5. So, bad comes from us and good comes from God. What is the good that comes from God in v 16-18 and how is it not only a contrast to, but also a cure of, the bad in us?

Q6. What is the part played by the 'word of truth' in the new birth in v 18 (see also 1 Peter 1 v 23 – 2 v 3) and how does this affect our ongoing relationship with the word? See v 19-25.

Q7. What are the visible evidences that the new birth makes a person like their 'Father'? See v 26-27.

'GOD BROUGHT A MESSENGER INTO MY LIFE'

Peter worked all his life as a carpenter on a building site but now turns his energies to evangelism among the elderly at the church where he came to Christ.

With his first marriage over and his children grown up, life seemed to take a turn for the better when Peter met an attractive divorcee at a dance club. But when the new woman in his life became a Christian, all that promise seemed to evaporate. Convicted of her own sin, she moved out of his house—and urged Peter to think about eternal issues, and invited him along to her church.

Aware of the abject emptiness of his life, Peter reluctantly agreed. To his surprise he found himself returning to the church each Sunday. Often he would sit in the meeting with tears of remorse streaming down his face as the gospel was preached.

As a result of attending a weekly men's Bible-study group at the church, he began to understand his need to get right with God. Life gradually took on a whole new perspective as the Holy Spirit started to work on his mind and heart. He found that he could no longer swear and blaspheme and that, quite strangely, he even began to see the need for his workmates to know the gospel.

He also began to appreciate that all the way through his life, God had been, as he puts it, 'knocking at my door'. Two years after taking those first tentative and unwilling steps to church, Peter was baptised. 'God brought a messenger into my life and then took her out again', says Peter, 'but the great thing is that as a result, the Holy Spirit also came and He will never leave me'.

7

"SURELY A LOVING GOD WILL ACCEPT EVERYONE IN THE END?"

The reality of judgment

Justin Mote

J udgment is perhaps the most unpalatable part of the Bible's message. Is it really essential? Or can we just smooth over it?

Not so long ago, I was caught by a speed camera. It was late and the road was clear, but I was doing 42mph in an area where the speed limit was significantly lower when I saw the flash in my rear view mirror. A few days afterwards the letter came. A £50 fine and three penalty points on my licence. My emotions were mixed. I was cross that I had been caught! I was frustrated at the punishment! I was embarrassed when telling my wife! But it was a fair cop. I deserved everything I got.

We probably all have mixed feelings about crime and punishment—particularly when it happens to concern us! The stark message of the Bible, though, is that we're all intimately involved with it—and on a more significant level than a speeding ticket. Our crime is against our Creator and His judgement is our present experience as well as a future certainty.

Present judgment is experienced

In Genesis we read of Adam and Eve's rebellion against their Creator. They broke the single rule that He had given them to obey (Genesis 2 v 16-17). They chose to believe the snake rather than the Lord who had made them. Chapter 3 tells us of the judgment from God as a consequence of this rebellion, a judgment on them and on their descendants...

We live in a world of physical death

God had said that they would die and they did. Not for some time, admittedly—Adam lived until he was 930—but his disobedience made it a certainty! It was Woody Allen who once said: 'I'm not afraid of dying. I just don't want to be around when it happens.' But he will be! For just as death came to Adam, it comes to all of us. And not just death, but decay as we live our lives in bodies hurtling towards that unstoppable conclusion, and experience the pain and suffering it brings to us and those we love.

We live in a world of spoiled relationships

All creatures are cursed, Genesis 3 v 14. The living creatures we were created to rule, we now have trouble taming. When we visit the zoo we are grateful for the glass that separates us from the poisonous snake. Further, human relationships are distorted.

In v 16, we read of marriage being affected. Marriage continues, but it is now hard work. In the next chapter we read of murder. Childbirth is painful (v 16), and the daily provision of our needs is through painful toil and hard sweat (v 17-19). And finally, mankind was cast out of the garden, v 23. We no longer live in the perfect environment God created for us. We no longer relate to the Lord God as He created us to do. The early chapters of the Bible explain the world we live in—a people and a world under the judgment of God.

We live in a world where we continue to sin

In Romans 1 Paul speaks of another way in which we experience the present judgment of God. He tells us in v 18 that 'the wrath of God is revealed from heaven against all ungodliness and unrighteousness of men, who by their unrighteousness suppress the truth'. The next two verses explain that God's anger, like His judgment in the garden of Eden, is just and fair.

God's anger is not a loss of temper or a fit of pique. God has made Himself known clearly in His creation. That is, no one can look at the world and not know, deep in their heart of hearts, that there is a Creator who designed it and sustains it, and more than that, who made each one of us too. And if He made us, we belong to Him. That's why God is rightly angry that we live our lives in His world refusing to give thanks to Him or to praise Him, v 21; in fact, for the most part, refusing to relate to Him at all! And so God's response is to 'hand us over' to the sinful desires of our hearts.

We live in a world where we reject truth.

Three times (v 21-24, v 25-26, v 28) Paul repeats this pattern of rejection of the truth about God, resulting in Him 'handing us over'. The dog owner will take off the leash from the straining dog. God has removed the restraints on us. He allows us to go the way we sinfully want. Our 'sins' are the evidence that God is angry with us and that we are under His judgment now. In the twenty centuries since the birth of Jesus we have advanced technologically, but not at all morally. In fact, some might argue we've regressed. Our 'sins' are the evidence that God is angry with us and that we are under His judgment.

We live in a world that is a mixture

A mixture of the good and the bad, the noble and the ignoble. Things are not as bad as they could be, but nothing is as good as it was created to be. All the suffering we see in our world, all the wrong we know in our own hearts, is our present experience of the judgment of God. And yet, in Romans 2 v 4 Paul calls it kindness. Kindness because we have not yet experienced the judgment we deserve.

We live in a world where God is patient

Partial, present judgment, whether it's our own experience of sin, or a disaster like the tower of Siloam (mentioned in Luke 13) or the locust invasion of Joel, is meant to alert us to the reality of what's ahead, and alert us to how truly awful it will be. And it provides an opportunity for repentance, so that we turn to God before that judgment comes. In fact in 2 Peter 3 v 9, Peter states that the delay in Jesus' return is entirely because of God's patience, 'not wishing that any should perish, but that all should reach repentance'.

No wonder Jonathan Edwards, the 18th-century American preacher, ended his famous sermon 'Sinners in the hands of an angry God' with this appeal: 'Therefore, let every one that is out of Christ, now awake and fly from the wrath to come'. I became a Christian on March 2nd 1976. I am glad that the Lord delayed Jesus' return and that he didn't come on March 1st.

Future judgment is certain

When Paul goes to Athens in Acts 17, it isn't the stunning architecture of the Acropolis or the Parthenon that he notices. He sees the city is full of idols. He is gutted that God is not being glorified as He deserves. He stands at the Areopagus and preaches. His conclusion comes in v 30-31.

Paul tells the Athenians that God now commands all people everywhere to repent. But why should people do that? 'Because he has fixed a day on which he will judge the world in righteousness by a man whom he has appointed; and of this he has given assurance to all by raising him from the dead.' Notice a day has been set. We have no idea when the day is. It is foolish to try and guess. But we can be sure that it will happen. Not even physical death can stop God bringing judgment on people. He has shown He has the power to raise people from death.

And so we can sure that all will be present. I recently received a letter from my dentist. I had missed an appointment and would be charged a fine of £5. The day of God's final judgment is one appointment that no one will miss. In Revelation 20 John has a vision of the judgment. In v 12 we are told that even the dead will be there. People will be judged according to what they have done. Everything has been recorded. And those whose names are not in the book of life will be thrown into the lake of fire, a lake of burning sulphur. It is the same destination as Satan went to earlier in the chapter.

It means that we can be sure that hell will be awful. Some people don't like the mention of hell. In the Bible, nobody speaks more about it than Jesus Himself. In His explanation of the parable of the weeds in Matthew 13 v 36-43, Jesus describes the 'weeding' out of the final judgment. Everything that causes sin and all who do evil will be thrown into a fiery furnace where 'there will be weeping and gnashing of teeth'. In another parable, the story of a rich man and Lazarus, Jesus describes the hell that the rich man enters. It is described as a place of torment, so awful that he wishes he could feel a drip of water to cool his tongue from the agony of the fire. The language is of ongoing, eternal judgment. And the rich man concludes by asking that Lazarus be sent to his father's house, where five brothers live. He wants them warned so that they will not come to this place of torment (Luke 16 v 19-31). Jesus' conclusion is that the Scriptures are warning enough.

Jesus speaks of the judgment to come, and the reality of hell, out of love. He wants us to believe Him. He wants us to trust Him and benefit from His death. At the cross we see Jesus take the full punishment of God's judgment on Himself. We hear Him cry: 'My God, my God, why have you forsaken me?'

Jesus received the judgment of separation from His Father, so that we might never have to face the final judgment. Although we still live in this world under judgment, feeling its pains, we can now be sure that 'there is now no condemnation for those who are in Christ Jesus,' (Romans 8 v 1) and that nothing 'will be able to separate us from the love of God in Christ Jesus our Lord' (Romans 8 v 39).

BIBLE STUDY

Read Revelation 20 v 11-15

This passage depicts the final judgment.

Q1. Who is the judge?

Q2. How is each person's destiny to be determined?

Q3. What are the only alternatives?

Q4. Whose names are written in 'the Lamb's book of life'?

See also Matthew 16 v 27; John 5 v 27-29; Romans 2 v 6, 16.

DISCUSS

Q1. Why do many people feel uneasy about talking openly about this subject?

Q2. Talk about some of the reasons why the idea of a final, perfect judgment is actually good news for the human race.

Q3. 'Surely a loving God will accept everyone in the end!' How would you answer this common objection?

Q4. What implications for our evangelism does this doctrine have? What is the message that we should be preaching (see Acts 17 v 30-31)?

JONATHAN EDWARDS 1703 – 1758

Sinners in the hands of an angry God

To many Christians, Jonathan Edwards is famous for one sermon which he preached in New England in 1741 entitled 'Sinners in the Hands of an Angry God'. Here is a flavour of it, as he warns unbelievers that they are suspended over the mouth of hell:

> "*This that you have heard is the case of every one of you that are out of Christ. That world of misery, that lake of burning brimstone, is extended abroad under you. There is the dreadful pit of the glowing flames of the wrath of God; there is hell's wide gaping mouth open; and you have nothing to stand upon, nor any thing to take hold of, there is nothing between you and hell but the air; it is only the power and mere pleasure of God that holds you up.*"

This sermon has made Edwards into a monster for many. But such a reaction to him is entirely to miss the point of the sermon, which is that preaching such a plain warning of people's plight is an act of love and kindness to them. Edwards was loving people by telling them their true situation. It is no kindness to someone who is about to walk over the edge into a pit to keep quiet for fear of disturbing their mind, let alone to deny that there is a pit at all.

This explains why in Edwards' work in Northampton and Stockbridge, and throughout his writings, we find a man who can expound the horrors of hell, and at the same time can speak again and again in his writings in the most moving terms of the love of God. Edwards knew that without the horrors of hell there can be no joys of heaven, since the greatness of God's love is seen in the terrible depths from which He has redeemed us. A man who rescues someone from stubbing his toe merits less praise than the man who warns another of a gaping pit open before him.

Hence throughout the writing of Edwards we find rhapsodic passages extolling the love of God against the backdrop of the infinite offensiveness of sin and the infinite punishment which it deserves, an infinite punishment borne in our place by the Son of God Himself:

"How they can sit and hear of the infinite height, and depth, and length, and breadth of the love of God in Christ Jesus, of his giving his infinitely dear Son, to be offered up a sacrifice for the sins of men, and of the unparalleled love of the innocent, and holy, and tender Lamb of God, manifested in his dying agonies, his bloody sweat, his loud and bitter cries, and bleeding heart, and all this for enemies, to redeem them from deserved, eternal burnings, and to bring them to unspeakable and everlasting joy and glory; and yet be cold, and heavy, insensible, and regardless!"

Treatise on Religious Affections

Such rhapsody in the love of Christ was a feature of his life and ministry. Here was man unafraid of true religious feeling, indeed committed to cultivating the affections of his flock to love Christ more and more as they considered plainly the plight from which they had been rescued.

Garry Williams

8 "MEN WITH A MESSAGE"

The priority of evangelism

Roger Carswell

The apostle Paul is a pattern-Christian. He is not our Lord, or Saviour, but he is a great example of what it means to be a believer. As far as evangelism is concerned, his example of strategic, fervent, faithful proclamation of Christ is second to none. Even at the end of his life, by his example, he was setting out essential principles of the priority of evangelism.

Paul had always wanted to go to Rome to personally preach the gospel there. Instead he arrived as a prisoner. It was not so much that Paul said: 'I must visit Rome' (Acts 19 v 21:NIV), but rather that Jesus had said: 'You must testify ... in Rome' (Acts 23 v 11), though Paul didn't know that he would be a prisoner there.

All circumstances were calculated to make Paul's trip to Rome impossible: the forces of nature, and the wiles of men and Satan were against Paul, but eventually he had safe conduct to the capital of the Roman Empire. It was probably his last journey. Paul repeatedly described himself as 'the prisoner of the Lord' (not the prisoner of Caesar, or the Roman guard, but of the Lord). And in prison we see that Paul was evangelistic to the end.

Evangelistic to the end

Evangelism is proclaiming the gospel to non-Christians who are listening. At the end of Acts we find Paul in prison under house arrest. There would have been restrictions but, at least to begin with, Paul was given great freedoms, which he turned into opportunities to make Christ known.

It would have been easy for Paul to feel that the situation was too difficult, and that he had already 'done his bit'. But instead, with a deep-seated recognition that men and women were lost, without hope and destined to hell, Paul had to speak. In Colossians 4 v 3 Paul asked for prayer: 'At the same time, pray also for us, that God may open to us a door for the word, to declare the mystery of Christ'. The prison door may have been closed, but it was an open door of opportunity, which interested Paul.

In Acts 28 v 23 we read three verbs which give us a clue as to what evangelism is all about. Paul explained, testified or declared and tried to convince or persuade. In verse 31 we read that he preached the kingdom of God and about the Lord Jesus Christ. The backcloth of all the Bible, and the foundation of all Christian belief, is 'Christ and Him crucified', and so our aim should be to pave the way to explaining who Jesus is and how He carried and paid for our sins in His death and resurrection. Then, we can testify as to what God has personally done for us and in us, and then persuade people to respond to the claims of Christ on their lives.

Ours are difficult days, with increased apathy and antagonism to the true and living God. But Rome at the time of Paul was not exactly eager to hear of their need to repent and believe. Similarly, Titus was not given an easy task when he went to Crete to reach the people and establish elders, in a place where the people were 'liars, evil beasts, lazy gluttons' (Titus 1 v 12).

When John Wesley arrived in the city of Newcastle he was appalled by the wickedness of the city. He wrote in his journal (on 28th May 1742):

> We came to Newcastle about six; and after short refreshment, walked into the town. I was surprised: so much drunkenness, cursing and swearing (even from the mouths of little children) do I never remember to have seen and heard before in so small a compass of

time. Surely this place is ripe for Him who came not to call the righteous, but sinners to repentance!

God knew what He was doing with Paul, for in prison, Paul actually found that his witness was expanded, enriched and authenti-
cated by his suffering. Tough as it was, Paul's evangelism was used
and people were converted.

Creative in his means

Paul became 'an ambassador in bonds'. He devised means to create evangelistic openings. First, he appealed to the people who
would at least listen to what he had to say. He called together
local Jewish leaders. We know too that he witnessed to the prison
guard, and that the message spread throughout the palace house-
hold (Philippians 4 v 22). He probably stood before the world's
most prestigious person, in the world's most prestigious court,
and faithfully proclaimed Christ.

Whenever the early Christians appeared before the authorities,
they saw it as an opportunity to witness! If it is true that the most
important message is that of Christ crucified and risen, then the
most urgent requirement for every Christian is to get that message out, by all legitimate means, to every person. Every aspect of
our lives is to have an evangelistic dimension, whether at work,
home, church, leisure or on holiday.

There will, of course, be a different approach to the various
people with whom we have contact, but the greatest act of friendship and kindness we can show to anyone is to tell them about
Christ, and introduce them to Him. We may have to fight the
temptation to cut ourselves off from contact and friendship with
unconverted people.

Biblical in his message

There is no special gospel for modern men. The same message,
which is the theme of the Bible, is just as relevant today as ever.
The authority for the message is derived from the word of God.

As we proclaim the gospel, we are not simply sharing an idea or philosophy, but unleashing a power, for the gospel is 'the power of God for salvation' (Romans 1 v 16).

God has promised to bless the proclamation of His word (Isaiah 55 v 10-11). I carry a Bible with me always, and as often as possible, I like to open it and show passages to the people with whom I am talking.

When the word of God is proclaimed either one-to-one or to a crowd, God the Holy Spirit takes hold of it and brings life out of death—new birth! This is what happened when Ezekiel preached to the valley of dry bones, and it still happens today when Christians get out the gospel to non-Christians who are listening. Remember that the sower sows the word. Peter wrote: 'If anyone speaks, he should do it as one speaking the very words of God' (1 Peter 4 v 11:NIV), and Paul instructed Timothy to 'preach the Word', not just homilies and jokes!

There may be different ways of preaching the Bible, (Luther, Calvin, Spurgeon, Billy Graham, Lloyd Jones—all preached the Bible, though they did it very differently to each other), but it must be the Bible which is being proclaimed. The Reformation was largely due to a copy of the Scripture left in seclusion in a monastery. There it was hidden until Martin Luther came under its influence, as its truths gripped him.

Our confidence is in the God of the Scripture to use His word, though our responsibility is to connect with the unconverted and apply the message. We have nothing to apologise for; nothing to be ashamed of, but everything to be bold about.

Fruitful in his preaching

The power in evangelism is the cross of our Lord Jesus Christ and the transforming effect of the gospel. Time and again, John Wesley would note in his journal at the end of a day: 'I gave them Christ'.

When we proclaim the word in a way that connects with people, we are:

★ sending out a light (2 Corinthians 4 v 5-6, Psalm 119 v 130)
★ planting the seed (Luke 8 v 1-8)
★ giving the medicine (Psalm 107 v 20)
★ wielding the sword (Hebrews 4 v 12, Ephesians 6 v 17)
★ serving the food (Matthew 4 v 4, 1 Peter 2 v 2, Jeremiah 15 v 16)
★ applying the water (John 15 v 3, Ephesians 5 v 25-27)
★ holding up a mirror so that people can see Christ and be transformed into His image (2 Corinthians 3 v 17-18).

We should expect God to do His work, and bring people to the point where they are willing to repent and believe the gospel. We sow, expecting that in due season we will reap. Needless to say, as well as the blessing of conversions, there will be opposition. It has always been like that. Jehoiakim burnt Jeremiah's scroll, cutting it up with a knife and throwing it into a cauldron. But Jeremiah

BIBLE STUDY

Read 1 Corinthians 1 v 17 – 2 v 2

Q1. What were Paul's priorities in his ministry, and his message?

Q2. Why did Paul feel so weak in approaching the task of evangelism, and where did he find his strength?

Q3. List the five types of people whom God has chosen, mentioned in the passage. What characteristics do they have?

Q4. List the things of which Paul was absolutely certain.

Q5. Why is the cross of Christ so important to God, to Paul, to us, to all?

kept on proclaiming the word.

Paul used the Scripture, even when speaking against those who were rejecting the word and the gospel. At the end of his life, in that prison cell, the whole purpose of his life could be clearly seen. Whatever else he may have 'done for a living', Paul existed to proclaim Christ.

Living to make Christ known and to win people to Jesus Christ, may not bring acclaim from the world: when we die, they probably won't put up a statue for us in the park; we may not even be in the obituary columns of the newspapers. In a hundred years from now, we may be forgotten, but we will have been involved in the greatest work—that of bringing people to Jesus. And that lasts for eternity.

DISCUSS

Q1. What are some of the things that force out evangelism as the number one priority in our churches?

Q2. Why do you think we find it hard to maintain an enthusiasm for evangelism?

Q3. 'Use opportunities as they arise.' Talk about some of the recent opportunities you have had to share something of the gospel with someone. Did they go well or badly?

Q4. What would encourage you to be more vocal or demonstrative about your Christian faith to others?

Q5. 'Creative evangelism.' We often think of the evangelist as someone standing on the street corner preaching. How is Paul's example an encouragement to us in this regard?

Q6. What practical steps could you, and your church, take

JOHN WESLEY
1703 – 1791

As a young man John Wesley went as a missionary to America but after 3 years returned to England acutely aware of his own spiritual need. 'I went to America to covert the Indians, but Oh! who shall convert me?' One evening in 1738 he heard Luther's Preface to the Epistle to the Romans, describing the change which God works in the heart through faith in Christ. As he listened he became aware of a deeper assurance than ever before that Christ had died to take away his sins and for his salvation.

From that moment, Wesley devoted himself to preaching salvation by faith in Christ as 'the very foundation of Christianity', along with his brother Charles and friend George Whitefield. Sadly, this great gospel message was not welcome in the pulpits of the Church of England, which was by then in the middle of a serious moral and religious decline. Wesley and his fellow evangelicals were not deterred and took to preaching outside in the open air—wherever people would listen to them! In doing so they were able to reach the mass of the common people, many of whom would never set foot inside a church.

Wesley travelled some 5,000 miles every year on horseback, up and down the land, preaching several times a day to the people he encountered. 'I look upon all the world as my parish. Thus far I mean that in whatever part of it I am, I judge it meet, right and my bounden duty to declare, unto all who are willing to hear, the glad tidings of salvation.' He would often meet opposition, not just from the Church of England but from all levels of society, yet he persevered and many responded and were brought into a living, personal knowledge of Jesus Christ.

Through the preaching of the Wesleys, Whitfield and others, Britain experienced an evangelical revival, which had a profound affect on the whole nation. Alongside Wesley's new 'Methodist' churches, other churches too were revitalised and, in due course, the evangelicals became the major group in the Church of England. The traditional free churches, which had also declined in numbers and vitality, were also revived and grew rapidly. There were also social and political changes as the moral tone of the nation improved.

Wesley's passion for evangelism never waned and he was still preaching in the open air at the age of eighty seven, shortly before his death.

James Burstow

SING TRUTH

O for a thousand tongues to sing
my great Redeemer's praise,
the glories of my God and King,
the triumphs of his grace!

My gracious Master and my God,
assist me to proclaim,
to spread through all the earth abroad
the honors of thy name.

Jesus! the name that charms our fears,
that bids our sorrows cease;
'tis music in the sinner's ears,
'tis life, and health, and peace.

He breaks the power of cancelled sin,
he sets the prisoner free;
his blood can make the foulest clean;
his blood availed for me.

He speaks, and listening to his voice,
new life the dead receive;
the mournful, broken hearts rejoice,
the humble poor believe.

In Christ, your head, you then shall know,
shall feel your sins forgiven;
anticipate your heaven below,
and own that love is heaven.

Charles Wesley

9 "HOW CAN I KNOW THE TRUTH FOR CERTAIN?"

The authority of Scripture

Christopher Ash

The Bible is the Christian's authority. All true Christianity rests on this foundation. But why do we believe this? And what difference will it make to our lives and our churches? These are the questions this chapter will attempt to answer.

Why do we believe in the authority of the Bible?

A Christian is under the authority of Christ

When I became a Christian, I gladly came under the authority of Christ. I took His yoke on me (Matthew 11 v 28-30). As a disciple, with permanent 'L' plates, I am to do all that my Lord commanded (Matthew 28 v 20). But what has He commanded? How does He rule me and my church fellowship?

Christ rules by His word, the Bible

Christian people who are evangelical (which means, 'true to the gospel') believe that Christ rules by His word, the Bible. The Bible is 'the sceptre by which Christ rules his Church' (Martin Luther). We may be confident of this for two main reasons:

1. The Old Testament: What we call the Old Testament was the Bible of Jesus and of His apostles. Jesus consistently taught that it is the trustworthy word of God.

★ In argument He appealed to the Old Testament as His authority (eg: Mark 7 v 8-13; Matthew 22 v 29; Matthew 4 v 1-11).

★ In shaping His life He deliberately fulfilled its prophecies (eg: Luke 4 v 21; Matthew 26 v 53-56).

★ He said it was inspired by God (eg: Matthew 19 v 4-5, where Jesus quotes the writer of Genesis 2 v 24 as 'the Creator said').

★ He claimed that it spoke about Him (eg: John 5 v 46).

2. The New Testament: In addition, Jesus made sure that the New Testament would be a trustworthy record of His life, death, resurrection and the significance of these things for us. He did this by means of a unique group of men He called apostles.

★ Jesus hand-picked them (Luke 6 v 12-16), taught and trained them.

★ Before He died, He promised them the special help of the Holy Spirit so that they would remember and correctly understand all that Jesus did and taught (John 14 v 26; 16 v 13).

★ They were witnesses of His resurrection (Acts 1 v 21-22).

★ After His resurrection He taught them further, especially about the meaning of His death and resurrection and how He fulfilled the whole of the Old Testament (Luke 24 v 27, 45).

★ God affirmed their authority as teachers in the early church (Acts 2 v 42) by many miraculous signs (Acts 2 v 43; 2 Corinthians 12 v 12).

★ Because Judas betrayed Jesus, Matthias was chosen to replace him (Acts 1 v 15-26), and later Paul also became an apostle (1 Corinthians 15 v 7-10; Galatians 2 v 8).

★ The New Testament books were either written by apostles or by those in their circle, who accurately recorded their teaching.

For these and other reasons, we may trust both Old and New Testament as the reliable testimony of God to His Son.

What does it mean to call the Bible 'inspired by God'?

The Bible has many human authors. So what does it mean to call God its overall divine author? It means that all the human authors wrote exactly what God wanted them to write. Paul says that Scripture was 'breathed out by God' (2 Timothy 3 v 16, usually translated 'inspired', though it really means 'expired'!).

But He did not breathe it out by a process of dictation. We are not to imagine Moses, David, Matthew or Paul sitting in their studies receiving signals from a heavenly dictaphone. No, they wrote in their own (very different) styles, using their own minds. Sometimes they were conscious of being inspired by God; often they don't seem to have been. But, as Peter says of the prophets (2 Peter 1 v 21), 'men spoke from God as they were carried along by the Holy Spirit'. Men spoke. But they spoke as the Holy Spirit carried them along. And so what they spoke, God spoke.

The Bible is God's chosen way of telling us what we need to know about Christ, ourselves and God's world, so that we may be rescued and live for Christ. He uses different kinds of writing to achieve this—story, history, proverb, poetry, vision, and others. There are many things (for example, about science or history) which the Bible does not tell us. But always we may be confident it is God's chosen way of telling us what we need to know.

Jesus Christ is God's final word to us (Hebrews 1 v 1-4). And the Bible is the rounded and sufficient testimony to Christ. There are many things we would like to know. But the Bible tells us all we need to know. It is both complete (sufficient) and completely trustworthy (inspired).

What difference does the authority of the Bible
make to us and our churches?

What does the Bible do to us?

Because the Bible was breathed out by God, it is 'the sword of the
Spirit' (Ephesians 6 v 17), the instrument God uses to change and
shape the Christian.

The Bible is God's instrument

- ★ to bring conviction of our sin, for it is the word of God who
  sees right through us (Hebrews 4 v 12-13)
- ★ to teach, rebuke, correct and train us in righteousness, that
  we may be thoroughly equipped for every good work (2
  Timothy 3 v 16-17)
- ★ to shape our church fellowships (Colossians 3 v 16) so that
  they will be full of real love and truth

The word of God and the Spirit of God

Sometimes Bible Christians are accused of turning Christianity
into a dead book, rather than following the living Lord Jesus
Christ. We are accused of being so full of 'the word of the Lord'
that we forget 'the Lord of the word'. But the Bible is not a dead
book. True, it does not change its words like the books in Harry
Potter stories. But it is the Spirit's book. The Spirit of God inspired
its writing, and the Spirit of God works in the believing reader so
that the written word is the living word of God. We do need the
Spirit. But we do not need the Spirit separately from the written
word to speak additional words to us. For He works through His
written word.

Challenges to the Bible: four rival authorities

Here are four common ways in which we are tempted to disobey
Christ by dethroning His word. Each rival is human rebellion in
disguise.

★ **Experience:** Here the question is: 'How do I feel?' If I feel that something is good or attractive, then it must be right. If I find it repulsive, undesirable or horrible, then it must be wrong. My authority is my feelings and emotions. Which means my authority is simply me, with my emotional side uppermost. It is rebellion against God, under another name.

★ **Reason:** Here the question is: 'What do I think?' If I think something is logical and fits in with my understanding of the world, then it must be right. If it seems to my mind to be unreasonable, then it must be wrong. My authority is my mind. Which means my authority is simply me, with my intellectual side uppermost. It is rebellion against God, under another name.

★ **Tradition:** Here the question is not an individual one, but a social one: 'What have Christian people thought and taught about this?' My authority here is not simply me, but it is still human, for it asks what people have believed, whether or not it is what God has said. It is still rebellion against God, under another name.

★ **Culture:** Again, the question is not individual but social. Here it is not a question of what other people thought or felt in the past, but: 'What are the values of other people now?' If most people around me think it's ok, then it must be ok. Again, we have rebellion against God, under another name.

All four of these alternative approaches have some value. We ought to use our minds (reason) because God has made us thinking creatures, and the Bible expects us to think. We ought to know God in experience (eg: Psalm 34 v 8). We ought to observe what other people around us think (culture), for the 'wisdom' books of the Bible (especially Proverbs, Ecclesiastes, Job) are full of such perceptive observations. And we certainly ought to take note of Christian tradition, for we are not the first to read our Bibles. But all of this must be under the Bible itself.

So the proper model of Christ's authority would look something like this.

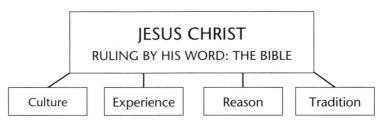

When culture, experience, reason or tradition gets the upper hand, we cease to obey Christ.

Each of these distortions gets into the Christian church.

★ Reason—where we take scissors to the Bible and cut out the bits we think irrational.

★ Experience—when we judge a church by the 'buzz' it gives us, or a preacher by whether or not they make us feel good.

★ Culture—where we are shaped by what our society thinks is acceptable, rather than by the Bible.

★ Tradition—when we ask what our own church teaches, or what our denomination's line is, rather than what the Bible teaches.

How will a Christian man show he obeys Christ?

1. He will read his Bible! He will open his Bible day by day and read it. He may use a Bible-reading scheme like Robert Murray McCheyne's to take him through the Bible in a year. He may use Bible-reading notes like Explore. But one way or another he will devour this wonderful book.

2. He will obey his Bible. He will put it into practice with God's help. Sometimes obeying a simple command. More often letting his character and values be shaped by God's. His Bible-

reading will never be purely theoretical but always challenging and applied to life.

3. He will feed on his Bible. He will rejoice in God's wonderful word. It will not so much be a rule book as a diet for life, the food that deepens his walk with Christ. When he feels spiritually dry, he will not look to alternative 'spiritualities' but feed more deeply on the word of Christ.

4. He will choose a Bible-teaching church where the leadership sit under the Bible as their authority. There are many bad reasons for choosing a church (eg: Do I feel comfortable? Do I like the other people? Is it my style?), but here is a good reason: Do the leaders believe that Christ rules His church by His word?

5. He will test preaching, Bible studies, Christian books, by it. He will not believe what he is told simply because he is told it, or because the speaker or writer is well-known, entertaining or persuasive. Always he goes back to his Bible to check.

6. He will test what he sings by it. He will not sing along just because he likes the tune or it makes him feel uplifted. He will ask whether the words put in his mouth fit with what the Bible teaches.

In all these ways Christian men will show that the authority of the Bible is a practical doctrine that transforms their lives.

B. B. WARFIELD
1851 – 1921

At the turn of the 20th century Liberalism was in full flow in the western church and the accuracy and reliability of the Bible was under immense attack. In 1887 B.B. Warfield followed Charles Hodge as Professor of Theology at Princeton University, USA, and, for several decades led the conservative evangelical defence for an inerrant Bible.

The church owes a huge debt to this brave scholar and preacher. Though vilified and derided by his liberal opponents and with only a few like-minded theologians on his side, Warfield wrote a score of books, articles and pamphlets to staunchly defend the trustworthiness, accuracy and reliability of the Bible.

In America the movement led by Warfield and others against liberal theology became known as 'fundamentalism', following the publication in 1909 of The Fundamentals, a series of brilliant essays that set out core orthodox Christian beliefs not only on the verbal inspiration and infallibility of the Bible, but also on matters such as substitutionary atonement, eternal punishment and the need for personal conversion.

A great scholar, Warfield helped strengthen the hand and heart of ordinary Christians by giving renewed confidence in the Scriptures and laid the platform for the advance of evangelicalism around the world in the 20th century.

Trevor Archer

BIBLE STUDY

Read Psalm 119 v 9-16

Q1. What is the writer worried about? (He is right to be concerned about this!) How does the word of God guard him against this? What about you?

Q2. What is the writer's attitude to God's word? If your attitude is less positive (be honest!), might this be because you aren't as worried about sin? What can you do about this?

Q3. How does the writer set about seeking God? What may we learn from this?

Read 2 Timothy 3 v 10-17

Q4. What is the choice Timothy is faced with (verses 10-13)?

Q5. How do the Scriptures help him make the right choice (verses 14-17)?

Q6. So why do you and I need the Bible so badly, day by day and week by week?

Real lives

"BORING, ODD AND IRRELEVANT!"

Before he became a Christian three years ago, the Bible was a closed book to Royston. 'I thought of myself as pretty clever. After all, I'd read the whole of the book of Job once at school for a homework assignment and thought it was awful,' he said.

'To me, the Bible was boring, odd and quite irrelevant, and I could never have guessed that anybody could take it seriously enough to base their life around it and the person it revealed.

'I hadn't, of course, banked upon God's grace in opening and changing my mind. I came to Christ after devouring Mere Christianity and quite a number of other books, including the first half of the New Testament.

'I examined the evidence for the historical accuracy of the manuscripts behind the translations of the Bible that we have, and was quite awestruck by the weight of it all—despite looking hard for potential problems.

'I had started to understand who the human authors were, why the books of the Bible had been written and, given the sovereignty of God, began to understand that it was God Himself that had caused these words to be captured. What's more, He had done it for our benefit. And eventually I concluded that it was quite legitimate to believe what the Bible said about itself: it is literally 'God- breathed.'

'So what does the Bible mean to me? It's the living word of our living God, providing His revelation of Himself to us. It's not a dry book of purely historical interest: it's a powerful, contemporary tool in the hands of the Holy Spirit, who inspired it. I'm constantly thankful to Him for speaking to me in such a tangible way.'

"TRUTH TO TELL"

The centrality of Bible teaching

David Jackman

However many or few books you may have at home, I guarantee that one of the categories most likely to be represented in your collection is the 'How to...' manual. The bookshops are stacked high with them—covering everything from golf swings to plumbing, perfect lawns to perfect marriages, training dogs to growing spuds and all stations in between.

I even have a book entitled, How to do just about Anything! But the 'just about' is significant, because it doesn't tell me anything about being a Christian. That book has already been written and it's still the world's all-time best-seller.

The Bible is the 'how to' manual on Christian living and discipleship. Its author, the Holy Spirit, not only has perfect knowledge to communicate the truth, the whole truth and nothing but the truth about everything that matters (2 Timothy 3 v 16), but also perfect communication skills to provide, within its pages, 'everything we need for life and godliness' (2 Peter 1 v 3:NIV), as we move deeper into life's greatest adventure—knowing God.

But it's not quite that simple, is it? After all, it was written originally in Hebrew and Greek. Twenty-first century men were not the immediate target audience, unlike our 'How to...' manuals.

The sixty-six books of the Bible were written over many centuries, by a wide variety of authors, in different literary styles and out of a great range of different cultural and historical contexts. Because each of the books did have an original target readership, very different from ourselves, there is bound to be the need for some careful interpretation, if the unchanging truth at its heart is to be distinguished from the cultural packaging in each of the books.

We need to discern the principles for understanding the Bible: the plain but precise meaning; the significance of its timing and context; the relationship of one book, or part to the whole Bible; and above all, the over-arching sweep of God's purposes throughout history, from the Garden of Eden to the heavenly Jerusalem.

Exploring God's revelation

At one level, the Bible is a book like any other, and if you can read a newspaper, you can read the Bible. But it has been accurately compared to the ocean, in its variety of depth. At the shore, it is shallow enough for a toddler to paddle in, but a little further out it is deep enough for an elephant to swim in. They are both ocean experiences, but there's a world of difference in their profundity.

And so it is with the Bible. The newest Christian begins to paddle, while the most mature will never be able to sound its depths or explore even a fraction of its incredible riches. However, the snorkeller can become the deep-sea diver! Everything depends on learning how to do it and that is why the Bible-teaching ministry of the church is so essential for us all. Let's explore the issue with three leading questions.

Why do we need it?

While learning-by-discovery is a popular educational method today, it cannot work in the area of knowledge about God. The problem is that God is, by definition, infinite in every attribute and characteristic, so that our finite minds and limited understanding can never discover or comprehend Him unaided.

We need God to reveal Himself to us, in terms that we can understand. And that is precisely what He has done in the written Scriptures, which point to the living Word, our Lord Jesus Christ. We all know people whose line is: 'I like to think of God as...' or: 'I can't believe in a God who...', but that merely makes them the central reference point of their world. In reality, they are not: God is. It is God disclosing Himself to us, in actions and words of explanation, which constitutes the foundation of biblical revelation, in all its infallibility and subsequent authority.

Central to the whole ethos of biblical Christianity is the need to receive and pass on to others the unchanging truth of God's self-revelation. All of us need to be taught and some of us need to be teachers. So the apostle Paul commissions Timothy, his 'son in the faith': 'What you have heard from me in the presence of many witnesses entrust to faithful men who will be able to teach others also' (2 Timothy 2 v 2). If, as Dr James Packer puts it, 'the Bible is God preaching', then we need that truth to be read, but also taught, explained and applied to every generation and every life-situation. The Bible itself teaches us that throughout its pages.

The first five books (the Torah or 'instruction', a better translation than 'law') are the Father's gracious revelation of himself to His children, in His character, promises and requirements. The prophets expand and apply those principles to the specific events and circumstances of the succeeding generations in which they served. Not surprisingly, there are nearly 40 references in the gospels to Jesus' teaching, which is His own declared priority (Mark 1 v 38). Teaching lies at the heart of the Great Commission (Matthew 28 v 19-20) and is the primary means envisaged for discipling the nations.

So much of the book of Acts is the record of the early church fulfilling that charge, going and teaching across the Mediterranean world, until Paul eventually arrives in Rome, at the heart of the empire (Acts 28 v 14, 30-31). One of the clearest apostolic summaries of this priority is Paul's double aim, stated in Colossians

1, where he describes his ministry content as 'to make the word of God fully known' (v 25) and his ministry aim as 'that we may present everyone mature in Christ' (v 28).

Letters of importance

The later letters of the New Testament were written at a unique time, when the apostolic generation was dying out, often taken through martyrdom, and when the churches faced an onslaught from distorters and false teachers. The letters of Peter, John and Jude as well as Paul's pastorals (1 and 2 Timothy, Titus), all underline that the teaching of the gospel and the true word of God remains the major task and responsibility of the churches, both to expose the lies and heresies of false teaching and also to promote and develop authentic discipleship.

The references abound—eg: 1 Timothy 1 v 3; 2 v 7; 3 v 2; 4 v 1, 6, 13; 5 v 17; 2 Timothy 1 v 13-14; 2 v 2, 4-6, 14-15, 24-26; 3 v 14-17; 4 v 2-5; Titus 1 v 9-11; 2 v 1, 7-8, 15; 3 v 8; 2 Peter 1 v 12-15; 2 v 1-2; 2 John v 9-10; Jude v 3, 20. Look them up and catch the urgency!

There is a body of divinely given truth to be conveyed, and it is central to God's purposes that it should be taught from one generation to the next. Teaching is central to the health and well-being of the church, whether in the congregation as a whole, or in its smaller units, by families, study groups, young people's and children's activities. The teaching of God's word is the central activity of the local church leader. Indeed, it is the only gift qualification that must be present (1 Timothy 3 v 2).

What does it look like?

Ephesians 4 is a key passage about the unity of all Christian believers in the truth of the gospel and through the ministry of the Spirit (v 1-6). But verses 11-16 build upon this foundation, with regard to the ongoing effectiveness of local congregations, (see the Bible study at the end of this chapter).

The role of the pastor/teacher in this passage is seen as the key to the life of the whole congregation, and every individual Christian within it. Without the consistent, regular and faithful teaching of the Bible at the heart of all we do, our congregational life will be anaemic and stunted, and our outreach will be lacking in confidence, relevance and penetration. So, the evangelical distinctive with regard to ministry is that the Bible's own emphasis is on the ministry of the word and that this is the pole of authority from which everything else in church life derives. On this view the Bible is in the driving-seat, setting the goals and objectives, teaching the means and methods, providing the resources and stimuli for all our serving, both as individuals within our families and workplaces and as congregations of God's rescued people.

In many local congregation 'cars', the Bible is in the passenger-seat, turned to for advice and encouragement from time to time, but not controlling the route or the journey. In others, it is relegated to the back seat (seen but little heard), while in some it is in the boot. But that is to imagine that we are in charge, that God has not spoken, or that this revelation no longer has authority, and we see the catastrophic results of this in church decline all around us. As Christian husbands, fathers, elders and members we must be men of courage and take action to turn this desperate state of affairs around.

How can it work?
Hearing God's word is, of course, a high-risk activity. Either our hearts will soften in obedience, or harden in rebellion, as a result. We cannot listen and then walk away unchanged, or imagining that we can be neutral to its urgent message. For 'the word of God is living and active, sharper than any two-edged sword, piercing to the division of soul and spirit, of joints and of marrow, and discerning the thoughts and intentions of the heart' (Hebrews 4 v 12).

So the proclamation and hearing of the Bible's message is neither optional nor peripheral, but central to God's purposes to transform us, as His people, more and more into the likeness of Christ (2 Cor 3 v 18).

The reason for this dynamic, or power, lies in the close relationship between the Bible and the Holy Spirit, which, for far too many years now, evangelical Christians have effectively separated. They belong together. The word was first given by the inspiration of the Holy Spirit (2 Timothy 3 v 16; 2 Peter 1 v 21), so that it is the channel and tool of revelation which God Himself has provided. It is the same Spirit who illuminates the understanding of Bible readers, as they ask for His light and submit to His instruction (1 Corinthians 2 v 9-14).

It is the same Spirit who empowers the enlightened believer to live out the precepts of Scripture and to grow in godliness (Galatians 5 v 16-26). They cannot be separated, whether in creation (see Psalm 33 v 6) or in anything else which follows. We are not, therefore, to see Bible-teaching as essentially cerebral, or just for book-oriented people who are well-educated. It is not a matter of intellectual ability, but of a mind that is open to listen to God, so that the heart (the biblical control-centre of the inner personality) can be set on fire with love for him and the will can then be energised to obey whatever the Lord, our God, is saying to us.

That is why we need to teach the whole Bible, word by word, sentence by sentence, paragraph by paragraph, book by book. They all count. But this needs to be done rigorously. A particular passage needs to be set in its book context as well as its whole Bible context. The detail needs to be interpreted in the light of the big picture themes of the whole, and Scripture compared with Scripture, so as to be able to develop a systematic view of all the great doctrinal themes of the Bible and their ethical implications, in a unified, coherent way.

This is a huge and demanding agenda, but there is no shortage of provision or supply from God's viewpoint. The question is whether we will take His offer seriously enough to work at its appropriation.

The 'How to…' manual is at hand, ready and available, but the challenge is whether we are willing to do the work. Whether in the pulpit or the pew, whether in the family, the workplace, the lecture or the church, the centrality of Bible-teaching, followed by learning and faithful obedience, remains the primary need and urgent challenge in producing rock solid, men and women of truth.

CHARLES H SPURGEON 1834 – 1892

"The prince of preachers"

Born into a Christian home, the young Charles spent many happy hours reading books from his grandfather's library. At 15 he was converted and one year later he began preaching.

People flocked to hear him and at just 19 he was called by a church in London to be its pastor. This was the beginning of 38 years of ministry, first at New Park Street Chapel, which became too small, and then at the newly built 5,000-seat Metropolitan Tabernacle.

From the age of 24 Spurgeon preached to a full church morning and evening, and hundreds were saved. He believed that if Christians were to live properly, it was utterly essential for them to be grounded in doctrine. In particular, he preached the absolute sovereignty of God. His published sermons were sold at the rate of 25,000 a week.

It was this focus on the greatness of God that led him to work amazingly hard. At his 50th birthday 66 organisations were listed which he was involved with, including his training college for pastors and an orphanage. He regularly worked 18 hours a day saying: 'We are not to be living specimens... but living sacrifices.'

Yet he knew incredible pain and suffering. His wife, Susannah, was a housebound invalid for the last 20 years of his life. He himself suffered from three different diseases. Perhaps most surprisingly, he suffered from severe depression. Although he hated it, he concluded that it was 'the design of God' to make him depend on God fully.

Yet he was a soldier for Jesus Christ who served faithfully. The combined effect of his massive workload and struggles meant that he died at just 57. But, in Lord Shaftesbury's words, he had done the work of 50 men.   **Ian Fry**

Real Lives

I COULD SEE THAT IT WAS THE TRUTH, NOT JUST SOMEONE'S OPINION'

Anton was brought up in South Africa in a nominally Christian family. 'We went to church every Sunday. I knew all the prayers, sang all the songs, prayed around the bed in the evening, but I felt there was no reality to any of it. I felt I was just going through the motions and I couldn't wait for each service to be finished.'

At high school, Anton came across a group of wild Christians and was keen to be part of their crowd, but although it was exciting to start with, his interest waned within a year. By the time he left school, he still called himself an Anglican but had no real faith and no relationship with God. 'I believed there was a God, but he was distant—not involved in daily affairs. And I was self-righteous. I thought I was good enough for this distant, impersonal God, whoever He may be.'

Despite this, Anton knew he wasn't living his life as he should and, when his grandmother died and he was confronted with death face to face, he chose to travel overseas in the hope that a change of scene would make him feel better. In London however, he found that he was still troubled and within a month of arriving he had accepted the invitation of a Christian colleague to attend a Christianity Explained course at All Souls in London.

'The CE course began with the reliability of the Bible and then took me through Mark's Gospel, step by step. I could see that this was the truth—not just someone's opinion, but God's word. And everything slowly started to make sense—I realised that the root of my problem was sin, and the solution to it was not drinking or travelling, but a relationship with Jesus.'

Anton remembers being struck by many Bible verses at that time, especially those that dealt with God's grace. 'Ephesians 2 v 8-9 and Luke 15 stand out in my mind because in reading them I understood that we are healed by grace, and that I needed to make a personal response to what Christ had done for me. I felt as if my eyes had been opened in the pages of God's word in a way that I had never experienced through formal religion. And unlike the experiential stuff I dabbled in at school, I knew that this was built on a foundation of truth in the Bible.'

BIBLE STUDY

Read Ephesians 4 v 11-16

Q1. (v 11) Which of these gifts were unique to the beginning of the church's life, before the completion of the New Testament? Ephesians 2 v 20 and 3 v 5 give us the evidence. Which are the continuing gifts?

Q2. The gift 'pastors-and-teachers' is one, as the original Greek grammar makes clear. How does this gift serve the whole body (v 12)? What will happen to the body if it is not exercised?

Q3. What is the goal of the building up of the body (v 13)? Unpack the ingredients of this verse and ask how far they are happening in your church. What needs to be done about it?

Q4. What specific dangers are we warned about in verse 14 and how does v 15a help us to understand God's remedy?

Q5. Why is all this not just 'cerebral' or intellectual, head-knowledge (v 15-16)?

Q6. What are the marks of the model church in v 16 and what is Paul's recipe for getting there?

"BORING, IRRELEVANT AND OUTDATED…"

The importance of the local church

Jonathan Stephen

Boring… irrelevant… outdated… stuck in the past… vindictive… hypocritical… out of touch… narrow minded… arrogant… dull… incomprehensible…

Ask any group of people in the street for their opinion of the church, and that's the kind of answer you are likely to get. But when we turn to the Bible, we get a very different picture indeed.

It is said of Christ that God 'put all things under his feet and gave him as head over all things to the church, which is his body, the fullness of him who fills all in all' (Ephesians 1 v 22-23).

Nothing, it seems, in all creation is more important than the church—because the church is intimately and indissolubly joined to Jesus Christ, and everything that happens in the universe is ultimately designed for her benefit.

God's wife

Why do we refer to the church as 'she'? It is because the Bible consistently describes the people of God as His wife. In an amazing passage (Ezekiel 16 v 1-8), the early development of the nation of Israel is pictured in terms of a young girl growing up. We read how, when she was 'at the age for love', the Lord entered into a marriage covenant with her.

This description of the Old Covenant (or Testament) as a solemnly-entered-into marriage explains why spiritual unfaithfulness is often called adultery. If the Old Testament people of God wanted to be spiritually fruitful, they needed to be intimate with Him. They needed to remember: 'Your Maker is your husband, the LORD of hosts is his name' (Isaiah 54 v 5).

The same is true for us as Christian believers. Just as 'the blood of the covenant' confirmed Old Testament Israel's relationship with God (Exodus 24 v 1-8), so the death of Jesus confirmed His relationship with the New Testament church. His atoning sacrifice on the cross sealed the marriage. That's why the apostle Paul wrote: 'Husbands, love your wives, as Christ loved the church and gave himself up for her' (Ephesians 5 v 25).

If we want to love what Christ loves, then we will love what He loves best—His people, the church.

An evangelical problem?

But how can we regard the church as Christ does? It's impossible for us to love every true believer of every age and place; the universal church will never be gathered together in this world, but only in glory (Revelation 7 v 9-10). Correct, but the Bible teaches that each local, gathered church is to be regarded as the universal church in miniature. In fact, this is the way in which the word 'church' is mostly used in the New Testament, much of which comprises letters written to particular, local congregations, explaining how believers should live as members of the church in the world.

It is largely because Christians in the west today are not sufficiently challenged about the relational aspect of Christian living within the context of the local church that they are so careless about its very nature and purpose. Both we and our leaders have become so attached to a culture of individualism that we are simply unable to hear what the Spirit is saying to the churches. Unfortunately, evangelical tradition may reinforce this particular problem. Our understandable emphasis on personal salvation easily spills over into the way we view the Christian life as a whole.

For example, we may regard the Sunday services as simply the most economic and convenient way in which the believers in a locality can gather to hear what God has to say to each of them as individuals. This reveals a serious misunderstanding of what church is all about. 1 John 1 v 3-7 is a good place to start if you want to appreciate the New Testament assumption that 'vertical' and 'horizontal' fellowship cannot be separated. In other words, communion with God and with our fellow believers are two sides of the same coin. Our relationship with the Lord must suffer if our doctrine of the local church is faulty or underdeveloped.

The essential local church

So, what is a church? We have always done our best to confuse ourselves at this point. We call the buildings where we meet 'churches', but they're not. We call denominations 'churches', but they're not. We speak of the 'church' within a certain geographical or national boundary—but that's wrong too.

I'm assuming in all this that we're prepared to let the Bible be our sufficient guide. One of the best, short definitions of 'church' is found in the old Anglican 'Articles of Religion'. Article 19 states that: 'the visible church of Christ is a congregation of faithful men, in the which the pure Word of God is preached, and the sacraments be duly administered according to Christ's ordinance'. The fact that this statement comes from an organisation calling itself 'The Church of England' may well expose an inconsistency, but doesn't reduce its value!

Although anyone of any religion or none is welcome to come into our buildings and attend our meetings, the local church, just like the universal church, is made up of believers only (1 Corinthians 1 v 2). At the end of Acts 2, the essential rudiments of church life are already clearly to be seen in the very first New Testament church, in Jerusalem. Verse 42 sums it up: 'They devoted themselves to the apostles' teaching and fellowship, to the breaking of bread and the prayers'. Nor did they hide themselves away. The joyful new community they created was, we are told, both very visible and highly attractive. As a result, 'the Lord added to their number day by day those who were being saved' (v 44-47).

The means and the end

We need to understand that the church is both the means and the end in the purposes of God. That is, the Lord has ordained the local church to be the means by which He will achieve His end, which is the universal church in glory. The New Testament emphasis on mission is not so much on personal witness as on the united testimony of the church. That is why God's word sets a premium on the unity of believers (Psalm 133). Jesus prayed that all who believed in Him down the ages might be one 'so that the world may believe that you have sent me' (John 17 v 21).

For this prayer to be fully answered, local churches need to acknowledge their obligation to express meaningful gospel unity with other like-minded congregations. This is perhaps another area in which we have failed to observe the New Testament pattern. Despite the problem of great distances, compounded by the difficulties of 1st-century travel and communication, the churches seemed to think it was vital to circulate information, share gifts and ministries, and meet each others' needs (eg: Acts 11 v 29-30; Romans 16 v 16; 2 Corinthians 8 v 18; 1 Thessalonians 1 v 7). The strategic importance of the local church is much diminished if it becomes isolated and self-absorbed.

The church in pictures

The Bible employs a number of startling images to help explain what she is and how she functions. Here are some of them, along with the body and the bride, which have already been mentioned:

The body stresses the life of the church, and especially the organic unity of church members and their Head, the Lord Jesus Christ. It makes plain that all believers need each other and must exercise their God-given gifts for the good of the church (Romans 12 v 4-8; 1 Corinthians 12 v 12-30; Ephesians 4 v 1-16).

The bride speaks of the responsive love of the wife for her husband. 'We love because he first loved us' (1 John 4 v 19). The picture of the Bride also powerfully reminds us of the purity and holiness of life that the church must always exhibit and maintain (Ephesians 5 v 25-27; Revelation 19 v 6-8).

The temple image reveals the church to be the dwelling place of God in this gospel age. The church is built, and continues to be built, as 'living stones' are added on to the foundation of truth laid down by the apostles, with Christ Himself as the chief cornerstone. That is why all true churches must be Bible-centred churches, where the truth is both preserved and proclaimed (Ephesians 2 v 19-22; 1 Timothy 3 v 15; 1 Peter 2 v 4-8).

The family concept indicates that church members recognise God as their Father and each other as brothers and sisters. Mutual affection and brotherly love should characterise any true church (Galatians 6 v 9-10; Ephesians 3 v 15).

The lampstand shows that the church continues the light-bearing role of Old Testament Israel. But now her light will not be hidden. The seven-branched lampstand in the temple is transformed into seven separate lampstands as the light is taken into a dark world (Matthew 5 v 14-16; Revelation 1 v 12-20).

Playing our part

Sadly, many Christians have never come to realise quite how significant and precious the church is to the Lord—and should therefore be to them. That may be, at least partly, the fault of the church itself. What the Bible has to say about the church, including the implications for the believer of belonging, is often not taught as much as it should be. To be an integral part of a living, praying, serving community—which is fed, guarded and guided by the Word of God in the power of the Holy Spirit—is no small matter, and none of us should ever regard it lightly.

Jesus said: 'I will build my church, and the gates of hell shall not prevail against it' (Matthew 16 v 18). Every true gospel church is living evidence that the Saviour has already robbed death of its prey.

Every true gospel church is the advance guard of the new creation. Troubled and tainted by the sin of this world she may be, but final victory is assured. It is the privilege and responsibility of every Christian to play his part in the great process. So, three cheers for the sentiments of the well-known ditty:

> Though perfect churches there may be
> Not one of them is known to me;
> And so we'll work and pray and plan
> To make our own the best we can.

DISCUSS

Q1. Discuss the negative and positive things you have experienced from belonging to a church.

Q2. Which picture of the church excites you the most (body, bride, temple, family, lampstand)—why?

Q3. How would you answer objections people have towards church? Are any of them true of yours?

'A PRIVILEGE TO BELONG...'

Cliff ran a print business until taking early retirement to devote his time to serving Christ in his local church—something he would have thought impossible 10 years ago!

As far as church was concerned, Cliff was a confirmed sceptic. He detested what he reckoned to be the hypocrisy of churchgoers and the scandals of 'the church' in history. For him, life meant being self sufficient, caring for your family, prospering at business and indulging a passion for classic cars. He wanted nothing to do with church, let alone Christianity.

Imagine his dismay, then, when his wife became a Christian! 'You do your thing, I'll do mine—just don't ask me to get involved' was his immediate reaction. However, after a particularly gruelling time at work he very reluctantly agreed to go with her on a church holiday, inwardly dreading the thought of five days with a bunch of religious freaks!

What he discovered blew all his misconceptions and prejudices away. Here were ordinary people of all ages and backgrounds who were very comfortable with one another and good fun to be around. Yet there was also a quality of gentleness and contentment about them that Cliff found quite overwhelming and intriguing.

Bewildered that his notion of church and Christians was being undermined, he agreed to go to a men's evening at which Martin Bashir spoke about his Christian faith. By now Cliff's world was being turned upside down.

Another home meeting followed where an evangelist explained the gospel, something Cliff had never really understood. Things reached a climax a few weeks later as he found himself in church one Sunday night under a great conviction of his sin and yet drawn to Christ and His people. That night he trusted Jesus and has since discovered how precious Christ considers His people and what a privilege it is to be in the true church!

D BROUGHTON KNOX 1916 – 1994

Broughton Knox was born and raised in Sydney, and studied at the London College of Divinity. He served as a Naval Chaplain in World War II before returning to Australia. He was principal at Moore College from 1959-1985, and had a profound influence on Australian evangelicalism.

Early in his ministry Broughton defended a doctrine which became a hallmark of his theology, that 'the only revelation is propositional revelation'. On this ground, Broughton held that the words of Scripture and the gospel are the only and entirely appropriate clothing God has clad Himself in to bring us saving knowledge of Himself. To be a person of the Bible is to be a person who is where God is.

'God wants relationship, not religion; religion is rebellion'. Because God works directly in the world through His word to bring us into redeeming relationship with Himself, God does not mediate Himself through human agency, even religious agencies.

Jesus is central: we are not fully human unless we are in union with Christ. Broughton stressed, therefore, that 'real life is fellowship'—relationship with God and each other. This trinitarian and christological understanding underpinned what is now known as the 'Knox-Robinson' doctrine of the church—that the essence of the church in the New Testament is not a world-wide organisation formed by Christians, but a local congregation, created directly by God through the gospel. Broughton was, however, no 'mere congregationalist'. He argued that the local church is nothing less than the physical and spiritual expression of Christ's person and work—it is the body of Christ. Thus, as a creation in and by Christ, it is to be characterised by listening to the living word of God, by faith, by edification and by love as it shares in the life of God.

Knox's perspective has been important in shaping the priority of the local congregation, and fighting the growing trend in churches worldwide for the denomination to take over the role of leadership.

BIBLE STUDY

Read Acts 2 v 42-47

Q1. To what extent are you devoted to those things mentioned in verse 42?

Q2. How might the example of the believers in verses 44-45 be followed in your own church?

Q3. How does verse 46 square with the modern complaint about too many church meetings? (And see Hebrews 10 v 25.)

Q4. In what ways do you think the Lord used the very evident joy and gladness of the believers to bring others to Himself (verses 46-47)?

Q5. What one thing do you think you could do to make your church more pleasing to Christ?

12 "HOW GOOD IS 'GOOD ENOUGH'?"

The necessity of holiness

Vaughan Roberts

Holiness, purity and self control are increasingly alien concepts in our modern culture. Yet these are the very things that we are called to as Christian men...

The consecration of Gene Robinson as Bishop of New Hampshire in October 2003 started a crisis which is leading to a split, not just in the Episcopal Church of America, but throughout the Anglican Communion.

Robinson is a divorcee who now lives in a sexual relationship with another man. Some hailed the appointment as a triumph for inclusivity and the all-embracing love of God. Opponents condemn it as an act of blatant disobedience to the clear teaching of Scripture. But the debate is not simply over homosexuality or the authority of Scripture. It also reveals divisions among professing Christians about the importance of our lifestyles.

One prominent advocate of the liberal position has said that what really matters when we look for a bishop is his belief in the trinitarian God—Father, Son and Holy Spirit, but 'how people conduct their lives in private is surely far less fundamental'. The Bible disagrees. Our God is a God of blazing perfection, who loves what is good and hates what is evil. There is nothing impure in

Him; He is holy. And He calls His people, those who belong to His Son Jesus Christ, to be holy too (1 Peter 1 v 15-16), in public and in private. The Apostle Paul in 1 Thessalonians 4 v 1-8 urges us to live lives which please God. We will notice five truths about holiness that emerge from what he says and then see his practical instructions on two specific areas: our sexual behaviour and our work.

1. Holiness is essential

'It is God's will that you should be sanctified' (v 3:NIV).

To be holy means to be set apart for God. As those who belong to Christ, we are already holy or 'sanctified' in the sense that we belong to His special people. But that holiness must then be worked out in practice. That is the sense of Paul's command in 1 Thessalonians 4 v 3. God's will for us, His people, is that we should live holy lives. This is not an optional extra; it is a command that we are all expected to obey. The Bible does not accept that what we think is more important than how we live. Belief and behaviour, the gospel and godliness, doctrine and disciple-ship are married in Scripture and 'what God has joined, let no one divide'.

2. Holiness is relational

'We instructed you how to live in order to please God' (v 1:NIV).

The fundamental basis of Christian morality is relationship, not rules; love, not law. We are not simply pointed to an impersonal code and told to get on with obeying it out of a sense of duty or fear. Rather, we are introduced to a personal God, who loves us and sent His Son to die for us. And once we have trusted in Him and received His love, we find we want to serve Him.

Paul tells us that when the Thessalonians were converted they 'turned to God from idols to serve the living and true God' (1 v 9). Christians are those who know God through Jesus Christ and seek to serve Him. So the fundamental question I should ask in any situation is not 'What do I want?' but 'What would God want?' Instead of seeking to maximise my pleasure, prestige or profit, I should be looking to do His will. How does He want me to treat my wife and children at home, my colleagues at work and my opponents on the sports field? How does He want me to use my money, time and abilities?

3. Holiness is biblical

'You know what instructions we gave you by the authority of the Lord Jesus' (v 2:NIV).

How do we know what pleases God? Paul replies with self-conscious authority: we should listen to his teaching. He speaks not as an ordinary man, but as Christ's chosen apostle. The Bible is not simply a human book. The Old Testament, the record of Christ's life and teaching in the Gospels, and the writings of the apostles are all God's word, inspired by His Spirit.

Occasionally a well-meaning person will bring me a cup of coffee after I have spoken at church. One look tells me I can't drink it: I am lactose intolerant and must avoid milk. They have tried to please me, but they have not. If only they had let me speak first and tell them what I wanted: black with no sugar. The same principle applies with God. We are bound to get it wrong if we try to guess what He wants. Instead we should listen to what He has told us in His word, the Bible. We are not free to reject its teaching as if we know better. Instead, we should study it, humbly accept what it says and then ask for God's help to obey it. Only then will we begin to please Him.

4. Holiness is spiritual

'He who rejects this instruction does not reject man, but God, who gives you his Holy Spirit' (v 8:NIV).

God does not simply tell us what to do; He also empowers us to do it. The holy God comes to live within the lives of Christians by His Holy Spirit (1 Corinthians 6 v 19). The Spirit gives us a new desire to please God and a new power to do so. Sometimes we feel helpless in the face of temptation. As we fall yet again for the same old sin, a little voice seems to say: 'You might as well give up. You'll never be able to improve in that area.'

But we must not accept that defeatism. We may be weak, but the Spirit within us is very strong. We should expect to change for the better. But it will not happen without our co-operation. It is sadly possible to ignore the instructions of the Bible and stop battling to be holy. That is very serious. Paul tells us it is to reject God Himself, who has given us the gift of His Spirit. Instead we should determine to fight against temptation and ask for the Spirit's help as we do so.

5. Holiness is total

In the whole debate over sexual morality in the church, I have heard a number of people say: 'I don't think God is very interested in what we do in the privacy of our bedrooms'. But that is another false division. Just as God is concerned with both our belief and our behaviour, so He calls us to obey Him both in public and in private.

Lord Melbourne, Queen Victoria's first Prime Minister, once complained: 'Things have come to a pretty pass when religion is allowed to invade the private life'. But God is the Creator of every day of the week, not just Sundays; He is the Lord of all parts of life, not just our overtly religious activity; and He sees everything we do, even when no-one else is watching. Another Prime Minister, Abraham Kuyper, of the Netherlands, rightly said: 'There is not an inch of any sphere of life of which Jesus Christ the Lord does not say "mine"'. He calls us to be holy at all times, in all places and in all aspects of our existence.

Paul's instructions in 1 Thessalonians 4 are representative of this biblical demand for 'total holiness'. In a few short verses he covers both the private world of sexual behaviour and the more public world of work.

Sexual behaviour

'You should avoid sexual immorality' (v 3:NIV).

The Bible teaches that sex is to be kept within the context for which God designed it: marriage between a man and a woman. Paul writes: 'Each of you should learn to control his own body in a way that is holy and honourable' (v 4:NIV). Where does that instruction most apply to us as the moment? Is there a relationship we need to break or a flirtation we should end? Are we fuelling our minds with lust through pornography or unhelpful thought patterns?

Self control in this area is very difficult. But we can help ourselves by avoiding people, places and situations which put us under the greatest temptation. One man moved his computer into the most public room in the house to stop himself from visiting pornographic websites. Another tried to avoid going on business trips alone and made sure he was accountable to a friend when he did so.

Work

The founder of McDonalds once said: 'I believe in God, family and McDonalds and in the office that order is reversed.' But no Christian should think like that. God expects us to please Him at work, just as much as we should do in church or at home.

So when some of the Thessalonian Christians were being idle, Paul told them to get working. Elsewhere he writes: 'Whatever you do, work heartily, as for the Lord and not for men' (Colossians 3 v 23). What difference would it make if we wholeheartedly obeyed that commandment? Would we treat the secretaries and the cleaning staff in the same abrupt manner? Would we still skimp on those jobs that no one really notices? Would we claim excessively for expenses?

6. Some final words of practical advice

All of us have failed to live as we should have done. We should ask

God for forgiveness and then resolve to keep striving to be holy. As we do so, let's make sure we get all the help we can:

★ **Study the Bible.** God's word reminds us of the gospel, which deals with guilt about sin in the past and provides the motivation to battle against sin in the future. It builds us up in our knowledge and love of God and tells us what pleases Him. We can't expect to grow in holiness without a regular diet of Scripture.

★ **Pray.** On our own we are very weak, but God's power is limitless. Let's keep asking Him for help, in our regular pattern of prayer and at moments of particular temptation.

★ **Work together.** Our wives and friends can be a great source of challenge and support. It often helps to be accountable to others in our areas of weakness.

★ **Start somewhere.** At times we can be so overwhelmed with all that is wrong in our lives that we don't know where to begin. We won't be able to sort out every area all at once, but let's at least resolve to start somewhere.

BIBLE STUDY

Read 1 Thessalonians 4 v 1-12

Q1. What are the greatest obstacles to us 'living to please God' (v 1)?

Q2. What will it mean in practice to 'learn to control our bodies' (v 4)? What hinders us? What would help?

Q3. What truths underline the importance of us obeying God sexually (v 6-8)?

Q4. When is it especially hard to love our brothers (v 9-10)? What will such love look like in practice?

Q5. How does our behaviour at work lose 'the respect of outsiders' (v 12)? What would win it?

'Called to be holy'

Akin is a Nigerian who has lived most of his life in Britain and works as a self-employed computer consultant

Although brought up in a Christian home and professing faith at the Christian Union at the university in Nigeria, Akin spent the next 18 years in England on a downward spiral of 'clubbing and chasing girls', that resulted in two 'illegitimate' children born to two different women. His life was in a mess, lived among the debris of the brokenness he had inflicted on others as well as himself.

Two years ago his second partner left him. Without his lover, his daughters and his job he was at rock bottom. Alone one afternoon watching a preacher on a Christian TV channel, Akin came under a deep conviction of his sinfulness. Hours of personal agony and desperation ended with a strong desire to repent and a recommit his life to Christ. A sense of the grace and forgiveness of God overwhelmed him.

Meanwhile, his partner had also become a Christian. The scene seemed set for 'happily ever after,' but in fact life has proven to be very tough. Talking with his partner at length and seeking mature Christian counsel, Akin has discovered that growing as a Christian means settling for situations not as he wants them to be, but as God in His sovereignty orders them.

What has this taught him? Akin says: 'Firstly to trust myself to God, He knows best. Second, that painful experiences are His way of teaching me to trust Him. And thirdly, that God's grace heals and brings you out stronger at the other end of life's heartaches and loose ends.'

J I PACKER B.1926

'Knowing about God is crucially important ... As it would be cruel to an
Amazonian tribesman to fly him to London, put him down without explanation in Trafalgar Square and leave him,
as one who knew nothing of English or
England, to fend for himself, so we are
cruel to ourselves if we try to live in this
world without knowing about the God whose world it is ... Disre-
gard the study of God, and you sentence yourself to stumble and
blunder through life blindfold.'

This quote from Knowing God conveys the enthusiasm and clarity
which has made Jim Packer one of the most influential and acces-
sible evangelical theologians of our times.

Born to working-class parents in Gloucester, he studied classics,
then theology at Oxford, where he was converted to Christ in
1944 through a CU meeting at St. Aldate's.

After we become Christians our next move must be to find out
how we might grow spiritually. This is one of the areas where Jim
Packer's work has been invaluable. Many Christians spend their
lives looking for an experience, a meeting, a revival, a teaching
which will instantly transform them into a mature saint, lifting
them to a higher plain of 'victorious living.' Early in his Christian
life, the young Packer was faced with this kind of idea.

But he found it divorced from real life, untrue to his own experience, and most of all, unbiblical. His discovery of the writings of
the English Puritans, who have shaped much of his thinking and
teaching both in Britain and (since 1979) in Vancouver, marked a
turning point. From them he learned that the path to holiness is

a path of self-humbling. There is no 'one-off' fix. We must rely on the power of the Holy Spirit in a daily battle with personal sin.

These words from Keep In Step With The Spirit are very perceptive:

'Repentance means turning from as much as you know of your sin, to give as much as you know of yourself, to as much as you know of your God (and as our knowledge grows at these three points so our practice of repentance has to be enlarged).'

Jim Packer has staunchly defended the inerrancy of Scripture and at present is involved in taking a stand against the gay agenda in the Anglican Church in Canada.

Tim Thornborough

Daily Bible-study…

Explore is a Bible-study devotional for your daily walk with God. Available as a book or as an app, *Explore* features systematic Bible readings from trusted teachers including Timothy Keller, Mike McKinley, Mark Dever, Graham Beynon, Tim Chester and Stephen Witmer.

Find out more at:

www.thegoodbook.com/explore

Contributors

Trevor Archer was lead pastor at Chessington Evangelical Church in SW London for many years. He is now the Training Director of the Fellowship of Independent Evangelical Churches in the UK (FIEC).

Christopher Ash is the director of the Cornhill Training Course in central London.

Roger Carswell comes from Leeds but was actually converted while on holiday in Lebanon as a teenager. For many years he has been a travelling evangelist and writer.

Richard Coekin is senior pastor of the Co-Mission network of churches in London. He is involved in teaching the Bible to workers in Westminster and in the 9:38 ministry training initiative.

David Field taught Christian Doctrine and Ethics at Oak Hill Theological College, and now works in executive recruitment.

Liam Goligher studied in Belfast and has also pastored Churches in Ireland, Canada and his native Scotland. He is now the Senior Minister of Tenth Presbyterian Church in Philadelphia.

Bob Horn was editor of Evangelicals Now and General Secretary of the Universities and Colleges Christian Fellowship (UCCF). Bob died in December 2005.

David Jackman is President of the Proclamation Trust.

Justin Mote is the minister of a church on the Wirral. He has helped launch the NW Partnership, and is also the Director of the North West Training Course.

Mike Ovey is the Principal of Oak Hill Theological College.

Vaughan Roberts has been on the staff of St Ebbe's Church, Oxford since 1991 where he is now Rector. He is involved in '9:38', encouraging younger people to consider the possibility of gospel ministry.

Jonathan Stephen is Principal of the Wales Evangelical School of Theology (WEST), and the Director of Affinity, an organisation promoting partnership between Bible-centred churches.

Tim Thornborough is the editorial director of The Good Book Company.

Dr Garry J Williams is the Director of the John Owen Centre at London Theological seminary and a visiting professor of Historical Theology at Westminster Theological Seminary.

Galatians For You
by *Timothy Keller*

The first in a brand-new
ground-breaking series, Tim
Keller brings his trademark
insights and real-world
applications to the book
of Galatians. Written for
Christians of every age
and stage, whether new
believers or pastors and
teachers, this resource
takes the reader through
Galatians.

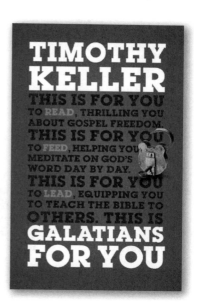

Galatians for You is for you:

- *to read* as a book, mapping out the themes and challenges of the epistle
- *to feed,* using it as a daily devotional, complete with helpful reflection questions
- *to lead,* equipping small-group leaders and Bible teachers and preachers to explain, illustrate and apply the wonderful book of the Bible.

Order at www.thegoodbook.com

Timothy Keller is Senior Pastor of Redeemer Presbyterian Church in Manhattan, New York, and the bestselling author of titles such as *The Reason for God, The Meaning of Marriage* and *Counterfeit Gods*.

thegoodbook
COMPANY

thegoodbook
COMPANY

Opening up the Bible

At The Good Book Company, we are dedicated to helping Christians and local churches grow. We believe that God's growth process always starts with hearing clearly what He has said to us through His timeless word—the Bible.

Ever since we opened our doors in 1991, we have been striving to produce resources that honor God in the way the Bible is used. We have grown to become an international provider of user-friendly resources to the Christian community, with believers of all backgrounds and denominations using our Bible studies, books, evangelistic resources, DVD-based courses and training events.

We want to equip ordinary Christians to live for Christ day by day, and churches to grow in their knowledge of God, their love for one another, and the effectiveness of their outreach.

Call us for a discussion of your needs or visit one of our local websites for more information on the resources and services we provide.

North America: www.thegoodbook.com
UK & Europe: www.thegoodbook.co.uk
Australia: www.thegoodbook.com.au
New Zealand: www.thegoodbook.co.nz

North America: 866 244 2165
UK & Europe: 0333 123 0880
Australia: (02) 6100 4211
New Zealand (+64) 3 343 1990

www.christianityexplored.org

Our partner site is a great place for those exploring the Christian faith, with a clear explanation of the good news, powerful testimonies and answers to difficult questions.

One life. What's it all about?